Hope for the Wobbly

A Treasury of Faith-Builders

Welby O'Brien

Lumen Harbor Publishing

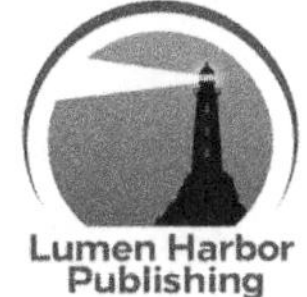

Hope for the Wobbly: A Treasury of Faith-Builders

Published by Lumen Harbor Publishing
Portland, Oregon

Editorial by Tamara Barnet

ISBN–13: 9781970897005

All images courtesy of Unsplash

Author photo by Keri Friedman

Cover photo by Aziz Acharki

Design by Robin Black, Inspirio Design

Welby O'Brien writes with such honesty and warmth, I feel like I've been walking beside her through the ups and downs of faith. What makes the book beautiful isn't lofty theology but its gentle acceptance of our frailty. This is a rare and needed message. She reminds us that faith can still stand, even when our knees are shaking.

One line stayed with me: "Perhaps He allows us to wobble so we will lean harder." That captures so much truth, that weakness isn't a sign God has left us, but often where His grace shows up most clearly.

Hope for the Wobbly feels like a kind companion for anyone in hard times. It points to a God whose strength meets us in the unsteady places, whose presence (not perfect circumstances) is the real miracle. It's a book I'd give to anyone walking through illness, loss, or just the quiet exhaustion of life.

~**Bart J. Fowler**, Psy.D. Licensed Psychologist

Hope for the Wobbly, filled with inspiring personal stories of joy and pain, will captivate your heart.

I love the way the book is organized—with chapter themes and a relevant prayer, followed by illustrations from everyday life, and brimming with faith-building Scripture.

We all need hope on a daily basis, and this beautiful book will give you hope. Why? Because the power of having a relationship with Jesus permeates the pages from beginning to end.

If you are a wobbler (and honestly, we all are), you will find this book of anecdotes to be a great resource as you continue your journey.

~**Dr. Terry L. Rommereim**, Retired Pastor and VA Chaplain

This inspirational book encouraged me in several areas of my spiritual and emotional life. It gave confirmation of how we all struggle, but there is always hope in Jesus Christ! I appreciated the book being arranged by topic, with a wide variety of short passages rich with insights. Some of the readings made me laugh out loud, took me to similar situations in my life, made me cry, or made me pause to ponder the truths shared. It's an easy read for those who want some daily encouragement in their life.

~**Brenda Kepart,** Ed.D

Welby O'Brien lightheartedly shares everyday experiences and aligns them with the reality of God's grace and interaction in our lives.

For those of us who have questioned God in the face of life's events, *Hope for the Wobbly* offers Godly wisdom and human insight in a manner that anyone can understand. The book introduces the existence of God into our everyday lives and his unfailing grace to all. And there is hope.

~**Susan Ruiz, PhD**, Christian Life Coach and Veteran

Now, more than ever, we need reminders that help us look for God in all of life's circumstances. Each of Welby's thought-provoking short stories takes us through her walk to truth, and her divine insights point us toward finding hope in our own daily tasks. She encourages us to nurture our spiritual wellbeing as one of the most important gifts of peace and self-care.

Whether you find yourself on a hill, or in a valley, these easy to read devotionals will inspire you to count your blessings, and listen for that still small voice that can and will help us through our day.

~**Christi Luby**, PhD

Welby is a woman fueled by her strong faith in God and her desire to help others. She has been a loving and faithful wife, and she has helped numerous people, especially those caring for someone with PTSD. *Hope for the Wobbly* is a powerful and helpful guide showing us all—whether strong or weak in faith—that God is always there for us. If you are struggling with your faith, this book is a must read; it will open your mind and your heart in your search for God.

~**Jan Catinna**, President, PTSD Projects

I so appreciate the wisdom and well-phrased empathy this book offers for what so many go through—such as poor health, invisible injuries, and even death. Each chapter has a combination of understanding weakness and strength through faith, with Scripture references for further support and encouragement. What this book offers is hope, and the strength of faith which can get us through anything.

I highly recommend *Hope for the Wobbly* for those who struggle, and also for those seeking to understand the wobbly friends and loved ones we strive to support.

~**Carol Ruplenas**, Blue Star Mother of Late Son

Welby and I have been close friends for many years. I've watched her go through all of the ups and downs that she shares in this book, and I've seen her grow in wisdom and love for the Lord. In *Hope for the Wobbly,* Welby reflects on the truths she has learned through everyday life experiences and the Bible, and shares in a refreshingly honest and fun way. She gives you a chance to stop and reflect on your own view of God, and the blessings He has for you personally.

~ **Cindy Gellinger**

As a "Wobbler" myself, this book is helping me understand how to overcome. I'd much rather believe in God and find out there's not, than not and find out there is.

~**Chad D.,** Iraq War Veteran

Welby O'Brien lives where you and I do. I appreciate her practical use of common sense in dealing with life's struggles that lead us to the truth of God's promises. This is a book that is easy to comprehend and helps us navigate life with strength and confidence.

~**Kathleen Benton**, Ordained Co-Pastor, Adjunct Professor at Colorado Christian University, and DCL Candidate at Trinity Bible College and Graduate School

I found the book to be highly impactful and enjoyable. Its practical insights and spiritual guidance make *Hope for the Wobbly* a unique daily inspirational reader, and also a powerful personal testimony that resonates with the experiences and challenges we encounter throughout life.

~**Dana Morgan**, Former President, Pointman International Ministries

What a book full of blessings! A few that especially spoke to me were a better understanding of how to face death—my own or that of someone I love, a renewed understanding of self-care as a gift from God, and encouragement to open our hearts and senses to a loving Father God. *Hope for the Wobbly* also inspires us to share the blessing of the gospel of truth with those around us who need hope.

~**Marcia Rigamonti**

I like the reminders that real hope comes from a relationship with Jesus, not a religion. For those who struggle with doubts, this book encourages us to never give up. And no matter where we've been or what we've done, anyone can have a fresh start with the living God!

~**Ron Leonard**, Chaplain and Pastor

Table of Contents

Introduction 13

Wobbly Sam 13

Chapter One: Eternal Perspective 15

I Really Need That! 16

Mortality Comes A-knockin' 18

What? No Religion?!? 20

Got a Cold Sore Last Week 21

Startling Dream About Betsy 23

How Is Your Gratitude Score? 25

As Time Goes By 28

Chapter Two: Wow... Really?!? 30

Thank "Gosh"? 31

The Portal Is Open! 33

That's All You Can Hope For 35

Fingers Crossed... Really? 37

A Gift You *Can* Refuse 39

It's That Simple 40

Chapter Three: Strength for the Journey 41

God, Please Fix This! 42

Feel Like Giving Up on God? 43

Strength In The Storm 46

Struggling to Find Your Footing? 48

To Those Losing a Loved One: The Gradual Goodbye . . 50

Waiting Is Hard 54

Chapter Four: Faith Boosters. 56
How Reliable is the Bible? 57
Undercover Daphne 60
Can We Picture God?. 62
Will Your "Truth" Wash Away?. 67
Trust the Pilot. 69
Teeter-Totter of Trust 71
Two Steps to Hope When Your Faith
Doesn't Seem to Work. 73
Chapter Five: Makes Ya Think 76
How Much Time Do You Have? 77
The Lifeboat. 79
Praise the Tree? 84
Two Mistakes People Make Before They Die 86
Island Sun. 89
Which Way, Lord? 91
Chapter Six: Surprises 92
Poinsettia Plot Twist. 93
The Richest Reunions: Looking Backward
or Forward?. 95
Mold-Hound Surprise. 97
Our Hearing Can Improve 100
Good News, Bad News 102
A New View. 105
Chapter Seven: Blessings 107
I Want Real Blessings! 108
Treasures In the Valley of Pain 110
Wardrobe Wishlist 113
Our Forever Helper—Guaranteed! 115

The Hungry Woodpecker 118
A Continual Feast 120
Changing Seasons: A New Take 122
Chapter Eight: Spiritual Self-Care 124
Self-Care Is a Gift from God 125
Saturate Yourself with Scripture 126
Pour Out Your Heart to God in Prayer 127
Fill Your Mind with Wise and Positive Input 128
Be Still... and Listen 130
Thank the Lord for the Blessings You Do Have 131
Chapter Nine: Tough Questions 132
Why Do Some People Curse God, and Others Sing? . . 133
Does God Offer Soul Insurance? 135
Can We Find God? 137
Birth Pangs and Death: Curse or Hope? 139
How Can You Say That God Is Good? 141
Halloween: Who and What Are We Celebrating? . . 143
Chapter Ten: Learning Curves 146
Boy . . . Did I Blow It! 147
Judger or Pray-er? 149
The Cry of My Heart 151
Three Tips for Reclaiming Joy & Peace in Turbulent Times 153
In Search of the Perfect Place to Live 156
Tapping into Supernatural Realms 158
Chapter Eleven: Heart Warmers 160
Puppy Love 161
Wanna Buy a Painted Rock? 163
School Is Almost Out! 165

I Love You Too! 167
Spring Is Coming! 169
100,000 Answered Prayers! 171
Chapter Twelve: Stress Busters 173
Word to the Worrywart 174
Take a Rubber Band Vacation 177
Want Peace? 180
Survival Checklist for Seasons of Stress 182
Save the Package 186
Be Quieted (with His Love) 188
Chapter Thirteen: Caregiver Kudos 190
Holding On to Your Joy: Can Joy and PTSD Coexist?. . 191
Faithful Over a Few Things 194
The Nozzle 196
Three Ways to Celebrate Love with or Without a Valentine. 198
Hope for Caregivers 201
Chapter Fourteen: Trauma Care. 203
The Three Most Neglected Areas of Self-Care During Trauma, Stress, and Loss 204
Your Name Here. 208
Reflections from My Recent Valley of the Shadow . . . 211
Stressed Around the Holidays? Here's Hope! 215
Who Cares? 219
Can You Get "Untriggered"? A GPS for PTSD. . . . 221

Chapter Fifteen: Fresh Starts 224
No Regrets 225
Can You Hear Me? 227
Sing the Scriptures! 229
GPS for Life 230
First Love 232
The Fifth Season 234
Chapter Sixteen: Timeless Promises 236
Salvation 237
Guidance 238
Peace 239
Hope 241
Epilogue of Hope: The Most Important Thing. 244

Foreword

With humility, humor, grace, and transparency, Welby O'Brien shares her faith journey—inviting us to come along and discover how we too can live life both wobbly and well.

Welby's collection shares truths of the Gospel message in a way that is thought-provoking. The theme of eternity-versus-temporal guides readers to consider life from a heavenly perspective.

Her personal experiences paint a picture of life that conveys: "It's okay to be human. It's okay to make mistakes. And we all have questions." Those who are wounded, discouraged, seeking more in life, or who don't fully grasp the immense love of our Savior, will find *Hope for the Wobbly* to be a refreshing book that leads to a greater place of discovery, acceptance, and growth.

Through her wisdom and words, Welby offers solid support and serves as a friend, encourager, and faith guide to all who are feeling a little wobbly in this topsy-turvy world.

~ **Michele G. Hudson**
Songwriter and Founder of
InspiredWidows.com

This book is dedicated to you.
May you be inspired toward
a brighter hope and a stronger faith.
God bless you! 🙂

Introduction

Wobbly Sam

When I was a wee little thing, our family doctor nicknamed me "Wobbly Sam." Must have been more wobbly than most!

Several years later, that same doctor sadly sent me home because there was nothing more they could do for my pneumonia. "All you can do is pray," were his parting words to my parents. And they carried me home.

Desperate with grief, they felt lost. Hopeless. Although considered good people and well-respected by the community, they had never felt a need for God, and knew nothing about how to pray other than saying grace at Thanksgiving.

So doing the best they could, they knelt beside my bed and cried out to God for help.

He heard. ♥

After I eventually recovered, my mom eagerly started going to a Bible study group. She soon learned about how our sins have separated us from God, and without that relationship, we are without hope. But the good news is that Jesus, the perfect Son of God, suffered and died in our place, to heal our broken relationship with God. And his gift of salvation is free to all who choose to believe.

She chose to believe and happily shared that good news with my dad, my brother, and me.

One at a time, we all also chose to believe, and began our personal journey of faith with the Lord. What a privilege it has been to have the Bible—his living guidebook and love message to us—as a foundation of truth and hope! Not merely wishful thinking, but assurance that comes from God himself.

My journey has been filled with blessings, challenges, and pain. I've had many wobbly moments. But as he promised, the Lord has been with me all the way.

This book reflects on many treasured moments from my personal journey that I hope will strengthen your faith as they have mine.

Perhaps he allows us to wobble so we will lean harder.

He loves it when we reach out to him in our wobbliness, trusting him to be everything we need. In the pain, in the struggles, and in the darkness—*he is our joy, our peace, and our hope.*

And the greatest hope of all is knowing that one day, when it's my time, my Savior will carry me safely Home to be with him forever. ♥

Now may the God of hope fill you with all joy and peace in believing, that you may abound in hope by the power of the Holy Spirit. (Romans 15:13)

CHAPTER ONE

Eternal Perspective

Prayer:

Thank you, Lord, that you are our hope forever. Please help us align our earthly perspective of time with your eternal promises.

I Really Need That!

Early in life, many of us discovered what we really need is that thing on TV, or what our friends got for Christmas. When our parents said, "No," we argued, "But I really need that!" (Never worked out for me!) 🙂

Those urgent needs gradually morphed into cool cars, hairstyles, athletic prowess, lucrative jobs, pets, a fit body, a nice home, fulfilling relationships, vacations. And the list keeps going!

The things we thought we desperately needed at the time may have been good things. It is normal to have needs and wants.

But what if we had to boil it down to one thing only?

As human beings, what is our greatest need?

Here are some answers I've heard: world peace, love, safety, education, plenty of food, good health, unity, family, conservation, freedom, comfort, financial security, happiness, etc.

Lots of good stuff, but it's an elusive task to pick just one.

And the greatest problem is that even if we were to have any or all of these, they would be *temporary at best.* Limited by time. Confined to this life alone.

What if God could offer the one thing that we as humans desperately need; the one thing that would extend beyond the limitations of this temporary life?

I often wondered why so much of scripture is devoted to God dealing with our sin, and ultimately displaying his great love for us on the cross.

Once I realized that our sin is our greatest problem, then our greatest need became clear.

Because of our sin (turning away from God), our relationship with him is eternally severed in the absence of his forgiveness. Therefore, our greatest need is forgiveness for our sin—salvation for our soul.

Regardless of what we may possess on this earth, nothing except his grace through Jesus Christ will free us, and it will carry us on to an eternal relationship with him in the heavenly realms.

And there we'll never again have a reason to say, "I really need that!"

For the wages of sin *is* death, but the gift of God is eternal life in Christ Jesus our Lord.
~Romans 6:23 ♥

Mortality Comes A-knockin'

It's always exciting to encounter a little drama on my routine morning walks. But this time was different. Up ahead I saw the flashing emergency lights of fire trucks and squad cars that had just arrived in front of an ordinary house I've walked by hundreds of times. It was a challenge to keep walking past the commotion, while also trying to find out what was going on without appearing to be a nosey thrill-seeker.

The police and firefighters immediately began hacking through the front door with an ax. As tempting as it was to stay and watch, I kept on.

And just my luck, one of the neighbors stepped outside to look, coffee mug in hand. "What's going on?" I inquired. Sadly, he informed me that something probably happened during the night to the older lady who lived there alone.

"Mortality comes a-knockin'," he mused.

"Yes, it does. And usually, it is not in our plans for the day. What would we do without the Lord for our hope?" I reflected.

So I continued on home, my typical light-hearted steps a bit heavier, saddened that all of us lose loved ones—and ourselves eventually—to mortality.

What do people who don't know the Lord hold on to for hope? Or is it just easier to say something such as "Mortality comes a-knockin'," and go on with the day?

I am so thankful that Jesus (whose name means "Jehovah is salvation") has paid the way for all of us to freely come Home with him when our date arrives. To exchange our mortality for his gift of immortality!

And all he requires is for us to choose to receive his forgiveness through Jesus his Son. No fancy prayers or religious rituals are necessary… just reaching out in faith to him to accept the gift of salvation he freely offers to us.

When Jesus comes for me, I hope my loved ones and neighbors will be able to say, "Jesus came a-knockin', and she was ready."

For God so loved the world that He gave his only begotten Son, that whoever believes in Him should not perish, but have everlasting life.~John 3:16 ♥

What? No Religion?!?

In the Garden of Eden, there was no "religion." Just **God—with man.** ♥

When man turned away from God, God reached down through Jesus to bring humankind back to himself. Jesus is Emmanuel, **"God with us,"** to all who receive him. ♥

Man has ever since been pushing God away, or hiding from him behind "religion."

In Heaven, there will be no "religion." Just **God—with man,** for all who have received Him. ♥

Got a Cold Sore Last Week

Got a cold sore last week. Approximately the size of Texas. In my younger days, I would have freaked out! But now? Nah. It happens.

Yesterday a stunning young lady caught my eye. She had it all: long purple hair, classic facial features, heavy glamorous makeup, cutting edge clothes, sassy salon nails, stylish tattoos, and a perfectly shaped body. Wow!

My moment of awe and envy soon faded as I began to wonder:

How much time and effort does it take her every day to achieve that perfect look?

And is it ever enough?

Does she think she's unattractive or unlovable?

Is she afraid to leave the house with just her natural look?

Does she dread getting old?

Is she happier than she looks?

Is her heart free to enjoy the peace, and joy, and hope, and unconditional love flowing from a relationship with her Creator and Savior?

I'll never know. But after many years of life, and seeing what happens to former movie stars, athletes, and all people, my perspective has changed.

How quickly the glory of the human body fades. And how tragic if that's all a person has.

I enjoy doing what I can to look good. But as time goes by, I feel less need to look great all the time. Yay! What freedom.

And the good news is that with every day that passes, when we seek God first and choose to rely on what he says, we're one day closer to our ultimate destination. It's an ongoing process to let go—to look beyond the temporal things that ultimately won't matter, and fix our hope on the spiritual things that have eternal value in God's kingdom.

I can ask, **"Will this matter 100 years from now?"**

I'm so grateful that God sees our hearts, and doesn't judge our outward appearance.

The cold sore is almost gone. I think next time I'll call it my beauty mark. 😉

Startling Dream About Betsy

Growing up I had a fun friend named Betsy. We rode horses together, talked about Jesus together, and even got in trouble together. 😉

When Betsy was just 19, she died from a bizarre illness. Shocked with grief, those of us who loved her took comfort in the fact that she knew and loved Jesus, her Savior.

Last night I had a startling dream about Betsy. I was in a public place surrounded by unhappy people. Suddenly Betsy appeared! Alive, radiant, and beaming with joy!

Beyond thrilled, I proclaimed to all, *"This is why we need a Savior!"*

And as we hugged, I woke up.

Wow.

I just lay there stunned.

For the past few weeks, I've been heavy hearted for those who have no desire to know God, let alone recognize our desperate need for him and his gift of salvation. And why would a person want God if they don't feel a need for him? "Seeing Betsy" as she is now with the Lord in Heaven—in lasting peace and joy, and very much alive—was my wake-up call.

The reason we all need a Savior is because we're all going to die. Either in sin—without God, or forgiven—with God. Just the truth. A fact we too often ignore, deny, or replace with something that feels better.

But what if each of us could fast-forward to our final breath?

Would we then be interested in a relationship with God? At that moment, we'd realize nothing else matters.

And what if each of us would open our hearts to receive God's forgiveness through his Son, Jesus our Savior? (Not religion or good deeds, which can never atone for our sin.) We'd know peace and joy and hope like never before—now, and every moment that lies ahead.

I'm so glad Betsy chose to put her faith in Jesus as her Savior way back there. Little did she know her last breath would come so soon.

He who has the Son has life; he who does not have the Son of God does not have life. ~1 John 5:12 ♥

How Is Your Gratitude Score?

I know a family who recently had a beautiful baby, another who just moved into a gorgeous new house, and a third who just became debt-free. They're all brimming with gratitude! But what about my friend who is lying in the ICU with cancer, and another whose wife just went on hospice, and a couple who just lost a child? Is gratitude just a fading memory for them?

For most of us, gratitude is the result of having a higher score of positive things in our lives than negative. Imagine that we chalk up one point for every thing that goes well, and dock a point for those that don't go the way we want. Then (and only then) *if* the good outweighs the bad, we can muster up some gratitude.

But what if our scoring standard is based on a faulty premise? Or at best something that's only temporary?

When I lost my father to cancer, I didn't feel very grateful. But gradually as the reality of God's promises and the solid hope of salvation started sinking in, my perspective changed. The pain was still there, but I was able to give thanks. Later I had the privilege of writing my book, *Goodbye for Now*, to offer practical help and hope for others who are losing or have lost a loved one.

More people than we realize are going through deep valleys of some kind. In those times, can we still be truly grateful?

Deep and lasting gratitude is not based on temporary situations, or anything we can touch or see in this world: bank accounts, body-image, health, politics, etc.

Our scoring system should reflect only what will last forever!

And whenever we pause (not just at Thanksgiving) to express thanks to God for his promises and blessings freely offered through his Son Jesus Christ, our gratitude score goes through the roof!

Studies show that gratitude not only affects our sense of well-being but also benefits our brain and entire body! 🙂

I love how the prophet Habakkuk finally arrived at the same conclusion. Braced for a brutal invasion, he feared they would lose everything, including their lives. Gratitude was nowhere on his radar! But after much wrestling in prayer, this is what he wrote:

Though the fig tree may not blossom,
Nor fruit be on the vines;
Though the labor of the olive may fail,
And the fields yield no food;
Though the flock may be cut off from the fold,
And there be no herd in the stalls—
Yet I will rejoice in the LORD,
I will joy in the God of my salvation. (Habakkuk 3:17–18)

And years later, Jesus instructed believers to "rejoice because your names are written in heaven" (Luke 10:20).

There's nothing wrong with giving thanks for circumstances or possessions. In fact, it's always good to give thanks! However, the deepest and most fulfilling gratitude is not dependent on fleeting things. We need to ask ourselves, "Will I still be grateful for this thing in 100 years?"

Is my gratitude based on joy that is temporary, or eternal?

The family with the new baby and the family who just lost a child can all experience genuine gratitude, if they know the Lord and have received his lasting gift of forgiveness and salvation. It is possible to weep and give thanks at the same time. One hundred years from now, our relationship with the Lord is the only thing that will matter—our true treasure.

And because of God's grace, regardless of what our earthbound gratitude score may look like, we are Heaven-bound and can truly rejoice in the Lord always! ♥

As Time Goes By

How did it happen that when we were young time just barely crawled and now it just zooms by? And how in the world did I wake up one day in my grandmother's body?!!

At the end of every year we celebrate the incoming new year, and also find ourselves looking back at the year we seem to have just looked forward to. The concept of time boggles the mind and is an ever-increasing source of frustration and fear.

God, however, is neither boggled nor afraid. He is the one who created time and space! Because he is infinite, he cannot be confined to its limits. He is the I AM. Always existing.

The good news is that he loved us so much that he limited himself to time and space, deliberately suffering the most painful death. Why? So that we would no longer have to be confined by time's cruel bondage. So that we could be his. He wants us closer to him than any other created being! He calls us his children, and his beloved bride. Even the angels marvel at this!

In the meantime, we are stuck here in these rapidly deteriorating bodies, helplessly watching the clock tick. Some of us are already admittedly in geezer mode, and hooray if we can keep our sense of humor!

The downside comes in the pain accompanying aging, the devaluation by a youth-worshipping society, and the fear of death. Those who do not have a personal relationship with their Creator and Savior can only distract themselves from the impending eternity without God.

But those of us who know our Savior have hope.
HE WILL COME FOR US.

If he truly is our hope, then time is our friend. It carries us closer each day to that event (which, by the way, is already on God's calendar)!

So, when I look at the date and wonder where the last fifty years have gone, or when I look at my grandmother's skin on my arm, I can laugh! I thank God! It's just more evidence that I will one day be in his presence, free from a sin-cursed world and the tyranny of time.

And that is a reason to celebrate! (Now if I can just remember where I put my party hat). 🥳

Absent from the body... present with the Lord!
(2 Corinthians 5:8) 💜

CHAPTER TWO

Wow, Really?!?

Prayer:

God of hope, thank you that in this hopeless world, you offer us everything we need forever. Please help us know you, the greatest treasure of all.

Thank "Gosh"?

I had no idea how treacherous the road was, 'til I hit an icy patch and slid out of control! Yikes!

Thankfully, I made it safely to my appointment. When I told the office manager what had happened, she blurted out, "Thank gosh!"

Wow… really?!?

Last week, a neighbor and I were admiring the gorgeous day and the stunning beauty around us. Gratefully I commented, "How can people look at all this and not believe in God?"

His response was, "…or *something*."

Wow… really?!?

I'm baffled. Why do people refuse to acknowledge God—especially in amazing moments that seem to be so obviously from him?

How sad. How empty. And even more so when they don't seem quite sure what they mean when they say, "or something."

I shudder to think where I'd be without the Lord, and I am forever grateful for the pure joy of reveling in his blessings! It feels so good!

Not only has God provided the way to forgiveness and eternal life with him in Heaven to all who choose by faith, but he is here with us now. And he delights in showering us with his goodness.

GOD is not just a "gosh" or a "something." Almighty God, Creator of the universe, actually wants a relationship with us!

And for me, a big part of that relationship is the privilege of thanking and praising him, and also enjoying all the gifts we so easily take for granted.

Ever think that maybe our blessings—laughter, sleep, food, hugs, good news, health, family, and every heartbeat, breath, sunrise, flower, and song—are invitations from God to respond?

Everyone has the privilege of choosing to respond to him by faith. Or not.

And right now I choose to say, "Thank you, Jesus!" 🙂

Rejoice in the Lord always. Again I will say, rejoice! (Philippians 4:4)

The Portal Is Open!

At about three o'clock on a Friday afternoon, a spectacular supernatural event took place. Yet most people have never heard about it, even many who were nearby at the time.

To appreciate the magnitude of its significance, we have to take a step back in time and view the big picture.

Most of us know that our Holy God created us to have a relationship with him, but tragically our sin severed that relationship.

But that did not stop him. He had a plan from before time began.

According to his commandments, Moses and the people of Israel built the tabernacle and later the temple. The daily blood sacrifices served as a graphic reminder of our sin, and the supreme holiness of our God. They never took away sin but showcased our need for a permanent Savior who would be the ultimate sacrifice and our high priest forever.

A massive curtain, known as the temple veil, was an enormous barrier to a very special chamber, the Most Holy Place. This could only be accessed by the high priest once a year, bringing blood on behalf of his sins and those of the people. There, above the Mercy Seat, God would meet with him.

Where was HOPE?

Where was the promised Savior who would break down the barrier and open the way to God again?

At about three o'clock on a Friday afternoon, the sinless blood-soaked Son of God willingly hung on a cruel cross. For you. For me.

"And Jesus cried out with a loud voice, and breathed His last. Then the veil of the temple was torn in two from top to bottom!" (Mark 15:37–38).

Hallelujah!!! The portal is open!

" . . . with His own blood He entered the Most Holy Place once for all, having obtained eternal redemption" (Hebrews 9:12b).

God himself ripped that barrier in two, opening up the only way to him. Why? Because he loves us and wants us with him. Forever.

Now he waits for us to enter. ♥

That's All You Can Hope For

Funny how you can chit-chat with neighbors for years, and then one day they say something that just floors you! Burt was out watering his glorious garden when I asked him how his mom was doing. "Well, she just turned ninety-two and has had a good life. That's all you can hope for."

Whoa!

Most people might have responded with something like, "Yep . . . glad she's had a good life." Or "Ninety-two? That's amazing!" Or "I hope I can be so lucky."

But to me . . . it's tragic. To think that this is all there is? And what about those who have *not* had a good life?

I shared with Burt that I don't know what I'd do without the Lord as my hope. He didn't like my response and went on to say he doesn't need God because he has mother nature.

Wow.

" ... having no hope and without God in the world." (Ephesians 2:12b)

This painful, lonely little phrase speaks volumes about those who have chosen to push God away and reject his free gift of eternal life through Jesus his Son.

The longer I live, by the grace of God as his child, and learn and grow through the ups and downs of life, the brighter my hope grows! The more this body fades, and the world around me fails to offer all I thought it would, eternity with my Lord is the sweetest hope I could ever have.

Because our hope is rooted in God's grace and trustworthiness, it is a solid hope! Not wishful thinking. But a sure thing!

This hope we have as an anchor of the soul, both sure and steadfast, and which enters the Presence behind the veil... (Hebrews 6:19)

And this hope is not just a future thing, but out of it flows joy and peace from a personal relationship with the Lord *now.*

You and I may be ninety-two someday, or 102, or we may not make it past tomorrow. I pray that you too will have the solid hope that only comes from God. ♥

Now may the God of hope fill you with all joy and peace in believing, that you may abound in hope by the power of the Holy Spirit. (Romans 15:13)

Fingers Crossed . . . Really?

What does God have to do to get our attention? With an unprecedented plethora of bizarre things going on lately, when people cry out for help, so many times God answers. Yet how do people typically respond? Here's what happened to me:

Our friends have farmland in Illinois, and like many they're dependent on the income from the crops. Two weeks ago I got a desperate email from them about the freak flash drought, and fear of losing the whole crop. I told them we'd pray fervently, and we looked forward to thanking God when the rain came.

Yesterday they wrote and told me it had rained! I responded with "Good news! Thank the Lord!" 🙂

From them: "Mother Nature has smiled on us."

Wow... really?

And then, "We'll keep our fingers crossed that the good weather will continue."

Wow... really?

Fingers crossed... knock on wood...? Yikes! We humans have a stubborn streak that sucks us mercilessly toward anything we can do to avoid acknowledging him as almighty Creator, and even more as our loving Savior.

Personally, my fingers are short and not in optimal shape, so I'm outta luck if I have to depend on them. Much less wood!

At this moment all I can say is God is amazingly gracious and patient to put up with us and our unbelief! And lest I be proud myself, I am thankful he waited patiently for *me* to open my heart to him.

Pretty sure God has done a *lot* to get our attention. And in his goodness, he permits reminders that we are not as in control as we'd like to think we are. I'm heartsick that so many reject him and his amazing invitation to have a personal relationship with us through Jesus Christ his Son.

They just don't want him. Period.

Rain or shine. Feast or famine.

Each of us has a choice: either we choose God and his way of grace and peace and forgiveness and life, or we reject him and eventually lose everything.

Perhaps that emptiness we feel in our lives—the sense that something is wrong—is a love nudge from God.

I pray every day that people everywhere will turn their hearts toward him. Rain or shine. Feast or famine. He waits with open arms. At least for a while longer.

A Gift You Can Refuse

How would you respond if you were offered a free gift card, good for anything and everything you would ever need? Totally paid for by the giver! Also available to anyone else who wanted one. No limits. No expiration date. The only requirement is that to get it, you have to ask for it in the name of the giver. How would you respond?

Here are some popular responses:

* *"That's pretty narrow."*

* *"I don't believe it."*

* *"I don't want to be obligated to anyone, just free to do whatever I want."*

* *"I insist on working for it."*

* *"I got my own thing going."*

* *"I can't receive that because I'm not good enough."*

* *"Had a similar offer...can't trust gift card people."*

* *"Maybe in a few years. Ask me later... "*

Or perhaps:

* *"Wow. Yes! Hard to believe, but I sure want that. And I want to know the Giver."*

God tells us, **"For the wages of sin is death, but the gift of God is eternal life in Christ Jesus our Lord"** (Romans 6:23).

Receiving or refusing the "gift card" and its giver is the biggest step of faith you could ever take, and it will determine where you spend eternity. Personally, I have no regrets. And the best is yet to come! ♥

It's That Simple

Imagine that right now, you're standing before Almighty God.

He asks, "What do you have that qualifies you to enter my eternal kingdom, and enjoy the glorious inheritance I've prepared for my saints?"

"Nothing, Lord. Just a dying body and a heart that sins."

"Would you like to be forgiven?"

"Yes, Lord!"

"My Son has paid your way. Do you choose to receive the gift of eternal life by believing in him?"

"Yes, Lord!"

"Welcome, Dear One."

> **. . . giving thanks to the Father who has qualified us to be partakers of the inheritance of the saints in the light. He has delivered us from the power of darkness and conveyed us into the kingdom of the Son of His love, in whom we have redemption through His blood, the forgiveness of sins.** (Colossians 1:12–13)

CHAPTER THREE

Strength for the Journey

Prayer:

Almighty God, thank you for your amazing promises, and that you will be with us no matter what. Please remind us that being strong doesn't mean we can't hurt or wobble during the struggle, but that we find our strength in leaning on you.

God, Please Fix This!

How much of our life do we spend pleading with God to fix things, change them, and make them just the way we want them to be? I know that much of my brain energy and prayer time is devoted to helping God know just how to do things for me. After all, I should know!

Recently it occurred to me that he knows way more than I do, and he cares way more than I can ever imagine! It's not my job to direct him.

Ask? Yes. Plead? Of course. But also trust. And accept.

And most importantly, walk with him in the path he has lovingly and wisely laid out for me.

Yesterday I desperately needed a walk, but it was pouring rain! As usual, I asked him to please stop the rain so I could go for a walk. He didn't.

Instead something much more beautiful and life-altering happened. I wrote it down:

I pleaded with the Lord to stop the rain.
"Please, God!" I cried, "I know you can!"
He didn't.
Instead he lovingly handed me an umbrella, and walked closely with me through the rain.

I realized that this truth has already carried me through many deep waters in my life, and there are likely many more to come. I pray I can remember that all he wants, and all I need, is to walk *with* him wherever he leads. Rain or shine.

Feel Like Giving Up on God?

Several people poured out their pain to me recently, one of them so distraught he wanted to end his life. Far too many are deeply wounded by life's tragedies! And even more tragic is that they all said they have no more faith. Everyone around them, and all their attempts to live well and pray, have failed.

I, too, have almost thrown in the towel during some painfully dark times in my own life. I've had seasons of rebellion, questioning, cynicism, and apathy. Just what was it that kept me from bagging it all?

For me, after struggling and searching, numbing, and trying to power through, I finally saw hope. Truth. Not just the best option—but the *only* one. And I have had decades to confirm it in my own life. 🙂

We all need the truth, and that is where I think our light of hope is found.

Here's how it all came together for me. From the very earliest days, the devil lied about God, and he also lied about man. And he has had a lot of time since then to destroy lives through the darkness of deception. Whether we consider our lives as fortunate, or if abuse or trauma or betrayal or tragedies comprise most of our past, our concept of God and our concept of ourselves have been profoundly impacted—and distorted.

The world and the devil perpetually seduce us with cunning lies—about God and about ourselves—many of which come from people we thought we could trust.

The most dangerous lies are that God is not loving and powerful and we don't need him.

If you have been betrayed, let down, been through horrific things, were mistreated, lied to, or abused, my heart goes out to you. The only answer for all of us is to do a reboot. *Stop.* Seek the truth. (Not popular these days, where everything is relative, and whatever you choose to believe can be "true.")

People say to me, "I wish I had your faith." And I always encourage them to just reach out to God. Rather than the quantity of faith, what's important is the object of it—that we choose to place it in *him*. Even the tiniest act of reaching out to him is the best place to start.

For me, and many others over the centuries, faith can't be contrived, but comes from hearing God's Word—*Truth*. That is where we will find the truth about God, and the truth about ourselves. It was Jesus who said, "I am…the truth… " (John 14:6). And also, "... you shall know the truth, and the truth shall make you free" (John 8:32).

The ultimate place where we see the truth about our desperate need, and the truth about God's love for us, is the cross.

The two true reasons to not give up on God have been magnificently displayed by Jesus on the cross. 1) We are sinners, dead and destined for hell without God; and 2) He is the answer—loving and gracious to buy us back with his own blood, so we can experience life far beyond what we can imagine, safely and gloriously with him forever.

Heard it all before? Sound like pie in the sky? Before you throw in the towel, I urge you to investigate God's Word, the Bible. A good place to start is the first two chapters of Genesis, the entire book of John's Gospel, and the last two chapters of Revelation.

The question is, Who are you choosing to believe?

In spite of all that's terribly wrong in our lives and our world, the two reasons not to give up on God are the truth of *who he is*, and the truth of *who we are.*

As a result of his love and mercy, and tremendous promises to those who are willing to receive him, *we have hope!* Not a religion, or a to-do list, but a one-on-one relationship with our Creator and deliverer. ♥

And when you're tempted to give up on God, remember he has not given up on you, but has shown you how much He loves you, and is waiting for you to respond. I hope you do. It was the best thing I have ever done!

Strength In the Storm

Have you been going through a rough time lately, or anticipate one coming? Recently hammered by one of life's storms myself, I came across this awesome verse promising to always give us all we need financially, stop stress, and bring beautiful sunny picnic weather.

Isaiah 25:4 begins:

For You [God] have been a strength to the poor,
A strength to the needy in his distress,
A refuge from the storm,
A shade from the heat.

Then I looked at it again. *Oops!*

I realized it did ***not*** say God would make the poor rich, remove all distress, stop the storm, and cool the heat. Bummer.

So just what does God promise for those of us who have chosen to believe him for our lives here and in eternity?

It occurred to me that God deliberately (on purpose!) created us to need him. 24/7. Why did he not just give us a lifetime supply of all we need, and take off? Could it be because he wants us near him? God created us uniquely for a living, growing relationship with him. 24/7. Forever. Otherwise, we might as well just be cactus. 🌵

When Jesus went through all he did on that cross, the separating barrier was ripped apart, and now by faith we have free access to God forever. He waits for us to just run into his arms!

The storms of life are lovingly designed by God to bring us closer to himself.

And now I see that ***he is*** the strength in our constant need. He does not remove the painful circumstances but instead uses them to draw us into his everlasting arms. *He* is our strength *in* the storms, and needs, and pain, and stresses!

I would rather have the storm any day—safe in the arms of my strong God—than have the sunshine without him. And I thank God I am not a cactus.

Struggling to Find Your Footing?

A weary single mom of four, overwhelmed with a flood of problems, was just barely making it through each day. When I asked her how she was doing, she cried, "I'm slipping! Doing all I can to find my footing!"

After praying for her, I gathered these scriptures about finding secure footing that have been a great encouragement to me, and printed them out for her to read whenever she needs that extra strength to go on:

- ♥ God is my strength and power,
  And He makes my way perfect.
  He makes my feet like the feet of deer,
  And sets me on my high places.
  (2 Samuel 22:33-34)
- ♥ You enlarged my path under me,
  So my feet did not slip.
  (Psalm 18:36)
- ♥ The Lord God is my strength;
  He will make my feet like deer's feet,
  And He will make me walk on my high hills.
  (Habakkuk 3:19)
- ♥ He will not allow your foot to be moved;
  He who keeps you will not slumber.
  (Psalm 121:3)
- ♥ But as for me, my feet had almost stumbled;
  My steps had nearly slipped.
  Until I went into the sanctuary of God.
  Nevertheless I am continually with You;
  You hold me by my right hand.
  You will guide me with Your counsel,
  And afterward receive me to glory.

Whom have I in heaven but You?
And there is none upon earth that I desire besides You.
My flesh and my heart fail;
But God is the strength of my heart and my portion forever.
(Psalm 73: 2,17, 23–26)

- ♥ Your word is a lamp to my feet
And a light to my path.
(Psalm 119:105)
- ♥ Jesus said to him, "I am the way, the truth, and the life. No one comes to the Father except through Me." (John 14:6)
- ♥ Now to Him who is able to keep you from stumbling,
And to present you faultless
Before the presence of His glory with exceeding joy,
To God our Savior,
Who alone is wise,
Be glory and majesty,
Dominion and power,
Both now and forever.
Amen.
(Jude 1:24–25)

For all who are struggling right now, I pray that the Lord will be to you everything you need! ♥

To Those Losing a Loved One: The Gradual Goodbye

I had no idea how hard it would be to lose someone you love—in stages. It's like they're already gone… but they're not. I always envisioned my dear mom going suddenly by a stroke or heart attack. What a shock when her doctor recommended hospice! Watching her decline steadily was heartbreaking, and the gradual goodbye was physically, emotionally, and spiritually exhausting. Here are some things I learned as I walked with her through that deep valley, thankfully led by our Good Shepherd and Savior.

Dealing with Reality

* There is no perfect way to do this.

* When we want to do more to help, maybe just being there is what they need most. Just *be* the daughter/brother/friend/wife, etc.

* Living every moment braced for *the* call is exhausting, and it's alarming every time the phone rings.

* There is no way to plan this. It's tough not knowing what's coming or when. We will have to cancel and reschedule a lot.

* The deepest peace comes from knowing they (and we) have believed and received Jesus as Savior.

* It's okay and necessary to take breaks without feeling guilty. Get away. Try to rest and regroup.

* Sometimes we feel pressured to prove our love, and wonder if we should be doing more. Pretty sure they know by now that we love them, and we don't need to convince onlookers.

* Remember that taking care of our own needs during this time is not selfish. It's vital! ♥

* They will likely be able to hear us even if they can't respond. Read to them as much as we can from God's Word to supernaturally comfort them and touch their soul.

* Floods of memories will come. Share the memories we are able to share with them, and cherish the others.

Processing the Pain

* Surprise waves of grief will overtake us. Let it flow.

* Even if it was a dysfunctional or imperfect relationship (most are), we still grieve.

* We don't realize how much grief is pent up in our gut until we get alone and let it out. We may need to wail. Often.

* As I wrote in my book, *Goodbye for Now*, **"Comfort is not the removal of pain, but it is knowing that with the Lord everything is going to be all right."**

* We grieve all over again with each new downward change.

* It's okay to let them see our tears.

* Celebrate the moments of hope, like realizing that in Heaven they will no longer need pain meds, wheelchairs, or doctors!

* Balance deep emotional releases (weeping and wailing) with breaks such as being busy (cleaning out closets, paying bills, etc.). There is a time for both.

* There are two kinds of sorrow: those who have no hope, and those of us who do.

* It's okay for me to let go.

* I can let go, because he doesn't.

Relying on God

* When we feel responsible and helpless, hear the Lord whispering to us, "The one you love is mine."

* We don't have to like it, or understand it. Trust God and love him.

* When people say, "Be strong," it doesn't mean we can't hurt or wobble during the struggle; it's encouragement to find our strength in the Lord. This is not just a physical, but also a spiritual, battle.

*** The more we fill our minds and hearts with God's promises, the easier it is to go on.**

* When we wonder why the Lord doesn't just take them now and avoid further suffering, stay open to all he is doing that we can't see. Trust his wise and loving plan, and his perfect timing.

* Keep your heart open to the special love messages from the Lord to you. Listen for your shepherd's voice.

* Tell them that when Jesus comes to get them, it's okay. They can go with him, and we will meet them there.

* We may not be able to be with them at the exact moment they go, and that's okay. The most important thing we can do is to walk with them as far as we can through the valley, and lovingly usher them into the presence of Jesus.

… and there we will never again say goodbye. ♥

Psalm 23

The Lord *is* my shepherd;
I shall not want.
He makes me to lie down in green pastures;
He leads me beside the still waters.

He restores my soul;
He leads me in the paths of righteousness
For His name's sake.
Yea, though I walk through the valley of the shadow of death,
I will fear no evil;
For You *are* with me;
Your rod and Your staff,
they comfort me.
You prepare a table before me in the presence of my enemies;
You anoint my head with oil;
My cup runs over.
Surely goodness and mercy shall follow me
All the days of my life;
And I will dwell in the house of the Lord
Forever. ♥

Waiting Is Hard

Eagerly waiting for my husband to return from an errand, my three-year-old granddaughter complained, "I miss Grandpa. Waiting is hard." So true!

Seizing the opportunity to turn this into a teaching moment, I waxed eloquent about babies who cry because they can't wait, adults who have to learn the hard way to wait, and how the Lord uses the hard times of waiting to do good things in us, and for us.

Anticipating, "Amen! Preach it Grandma!" on her part, instead I got a, "What's that?" LOL! 🙂

Nobody likes to wait. Whether for finances to improve, relationships to mend, illnesses to heal, and so on. And that is probably why all through scripture, the Lord speaks to us about it. It *is* hard. And no fun. We do all we can to try to speed things up. Even more so now in this instant on-demand generation.

I think waiting is at the heart of faith, and faith at the heart of waiting.

God could have easily put us in fast-forward mode, but he deliberately designed us to have to wait—for almost everything that is good.

If we look back at all the times when we had to rely totally on him and his promises, and proceed in the dark, we might be surprised that things actually turned out okay. And how we may have even emerged stronger, more fruitful, and closer to him because of it all.

When we wait in faith, trusting God to do as he has said,

it pleases him, and keeps us close to him... which is where we were originally created to be. Deeply and fully satisfied.

The bottom line of our hope and our salvation rests in waiting. Faith is going forward with life in spite of not seeing what we are counting on.

Relying on the shed blood of Jesus the Son of God on the cross for our sin, and banking on the eventual realization of his promises awaiting us, we take steps of faith one day at a time.

Interesting that in the Hebrew language "wait" is an active (not passive) word. It means to *wait with anticipation.* I love this scripture reminding us that although we all have to wait, the day will come when we will rejoice in the Lord, and see and experience all we have based our lives on. No more waiting. Just celebrating!

Rest assured that it will be well worth the wait! 

And it will be said in that day:
"Behold, this is our God;
We have waited for Him, and He will save us.
This is the LORD;
We have waited for Him;
We will be glad and rejoice in His salvation."
~Isaiah 25:9

CHAPTER FOUR

Faith Boosters

Prayer:

Open my eyes, Lord, to see everything you want me to see, and trust you for what you don't want me to see.

How Reliable Is the Bible?

With so many conflicting claims to truth vying for our trust, how do we sort through the clamor and ultimately land on the right one—the only one on which we can confidently bank our lives and our eternal destiny?

When my faith starts to wobble, it helps to be reminded of a few facts about the reliability of the Bible.

1. The Bible has been accurately preserved for thousands of years.

No other ancient document has as much physical evidence supporting its reliability. Just one example is the 1947 discovery of the Dead Sea Scrolls, which verified over a thousand years of scriptural accuracy.

2. The Bible contains a consistent message.

What are the odds of forty different people on three continents—most of whom lived at different times and didn't know each other, writing over a period of 1500 years—all being in agreement with one another?

I love how author Kathy Howard puts it:

"All the individual books and stories within the Bible join together to tell us one big story. From Genesis to Revelation we read the golden thread of God's rule, reign, and redemptive purposes. Jesus is present from the first story until the last. We call this God's Big story or the 'meta-narrative' of scripture. The presence of this meta-narrative proves God's design, control, and intent. It shows us that we can trust what God has preserved for us."

(KathyHoward.org, accessed October 2025, https://www.kathyhoward.org/3-reasons-we-can-trust-the-bible/)

3. The Bible has a perfect track record of fulfilling prophecy.

Astrophysicist Hugh Ross reveals stunning mathematical odds for the Bible's uniqueness in accurately foretelling specific events in detail, far in advance of their occurrence. He states that of the approximately 2,500 prophecies in the Bible, about 2,000 have already been fulfilled to the letter—no errors.

Ross (Reasons.org, accessed October 2025) goes on to say, "The remaining 500 or so reach into the future and may be seen unfolding as days go by. Since the probability for any one of these prophecies having been fulfilled by chance averages less than one in ten (figured very conservatively) and since the prophecies are for the most part independent of one another, the odds for all these prophecies having been fulfilled by chance without error is less than one in 10^{2000} (that is 1 with 2,000 zeros written after it)!"

For more astounding details, see: https://reasons.org/explore/publications/articles/fulfilled-prophecy-evidence-for-the-reliability-of-the-bible (by Hugh Ross)

#4. The Bible documents overwhelming evidence of the resurrection of Jesus Christ.

This is one of my favorites when I'm feeling rattled by doubts. Jesus Christ fulfilled over 300 specific prophecies from scripture. All of them! And during his time on earth, Jesus told his disciples that he would suffer and die, and then rise again.

Here are a few historically documented facts:

- Jesus was a real person who lived and was crucified.
- The people who wrote about him in the gospel accounts (Matthew, Mark, Luke and John) were eyewitnesses, or living at the time.
- Even his enemies acknowledged that his dead body had been in the tomb and three days later it was gone.
- Over 500 witnesses saw him alive over the next forty days.
- Ten of his disciples willingly died as martyrs for their faith.

#5. God has given us his Word because he wants us.

Remember the big picture. The Bible has been given to us to help us come to know him as our Savior and Lord, to strengthen our faith, and to equip us with everything we need for our journey.

This is God's love letter to you. Ask him to help you understand his truth every time you read it. He loves you more than you can imagine. And his love is reliable! ♥

~~~~~~~~~~~~~~~~

Books to consider:
The Case for Christ by Lee Strobel
Evidence that Demands a Verdict by Josh McDowell and Sean McDowell

~~~~~~~~~~~~~~~~

Undercover Daphne

Last year, Welby brought me home and lovingly planted me. She'd been longing for a daphne of her own, to one day bring her the joy of fragrant blooms heralding the onset of spring.

Every day she tenderly watered me, nurtured me, and talked to me. Our moments together were the highlight of my days! I was so happy and grateful. 🙂

Then one bitter cold day I awoke suddenly to terrifying darkness. Shivering and shaking in the howling wind, I could see no light at all. Where was she? What was happening?

I felt alone. Frightened. Abandoned. As hard as I tried, I couldn't understand.

Didn't she know what I needed? Did she no longer love me, or was she just not able to take care of me anymore?

Angrily I cried out, "It isn't fair!"

It seemed like an eternity. The sun never came up. I lost track of the days in the freezing darkness.

I wasn't sure which was worse… being alone or being in pain. I wondered how I could go on.

Then suddenly one morning the sky lit up with dazzling brightness! And there she was! Close to tears, she knelt down in the snow to see how I was. I was alive!

Soon I saw her carrying away a dark bucket. Overflowing with gratitude, I realized it had been sheltering me from the bitter blizzard. 💙

I'm still healing from my bruises, and I may always have scars. But I am blooming! And perhaps the blossoms are even more glorious because of the storm, and because I was lovingly cared for by the one who truly did know what was best for me.

I hope to always remember that I don't have to understand to trust.

(PS: Guess what's bringing joy in a crystal vase right now?) 

And we know that all things work together for good to those who love God, to those who are the called according to *His* purpose. (Romans 8:28)

❧

Can We Picture God?

All my life I've tried to picture God. Is he way high up in the sky? Or floating around us like an invisible vapor, or still hanging on a cross? Some may say God is nature, or the universe.

Why is it so hard for us to envision God? And how do we make him feel closer and more real as we approach him in worship and prayer?

As humans, many of us struggle with these concepts. God loves that we desire to draw near to him in faith, especially with our honest questions.

Throughout history, countless artists have attempted to portray images of deity. How would it even be possible to reduce a spirit being of infinite dimensions to a canvas or statue? The truth about God is not contrived by our sin-stained human minds, nor dependent on fluctuating feelings. And any attempts we make to depict him visually are distracting, inaccurate, and fail miserably at portraying an infinite Holy Almighty God.

An accurate concept of God must be based on the truth of his Word—all that he has revealed to us in the Bible.

Another reason we struggle to see and feel the Lord is that the limitations of our five senses and our three-dimensional earthbound bodies aren't capable of seeing God, or even imagining him in all his glory.

We can't reduce an infinite Almighty God to something our senses can detect or perceive.

How would you describe a glorious sunset or a star-studded night sky to someone born blind?

I love this description:

> [God], who alone has immortality, dwelling in unapproachable light, whom no man has seen or can see, to whom *be* honor and everlasting power. Amen. (1 Timothy 6:16)

Despite the immensity of God and his glory contrasted with our glaring limitations, the good news is that he has made a way for us to know him, and to catch a partial glimpse of him. There are three contemplations that have been especially helpful to me in my faith-walk with the Lord.

1. God Reveals Who He Is Through His Creation and Through His Son

Through Creation:

> For since the creation of the world His invisible *attributes* are clearly seen, being understood by the things that are made, *even* His eternal power and Godhead. (Romans 1:20a)

Every time we marvel at a glowing sunset, or thrill at a rushing river or rolling waves, are dazzled by a brilliant rainbow, or savor the fragrance of a flower or the pleasure of good food, or waken to early morning songbirds, or hold a newborn baby… give him glory! In that beautiful moment, our hearts draw close to him as we praise our loving, amazing Creator!

Through his Son, Jesus Christ:

> No one has seen God at any time. The only begotten Son, who is in the bosom of the Father, He has declared *Him*. (John 1:18)
>
> [*His* Son], who being the brightness of His glory and the express image of His person. (Hebrews 1:3)

The best way to know God is to know Jesus.

2. God Provides Two Ways to Personally Interact with Him: Worship/Thanksgiving, and Requests/Needs

Throughout scripture, we see that God desires our heartfelt worship and the outpouring of our needs. This is a prayer Jesus taught us. We always start with worship—acknowledging who he is and his holiness—and then ask for what we need.

> Our Father in heaven,
> Hallowed be Your name.
> Your kingdom come.
> Your will be done
> On earth as *it is* in heaven.
>
> Give us this day our daily bread.
> And forgive us our debts,
> As we forgive our debtors.
> And do not lead us into temptation,
> But deliver us from the evil one.
> For Yours is the kingdom and the power and the glory forever. Amen. (Matthew 6:9–13)

Our Worship:

God is spirit. When we reach out to him from the depths of our heart, it is an honest and spiritual interaction. (See John: Chapter 4)

God's holiness is the focal point of worship (both from us and from the angelic beings).

And one cried to another and said:

> "Holy, holy, holy is the LORD of hosts;
> The whole earth is full of His glory!"
> (Isaiah 6:3)

Our Needs:

Because Jesus is our Great High Priest, we can come to him anytime. One thing that can help when we pray is to focus on his attributes/names one at a time:

When I need care and rest, he is my Good Shepherd. (See John 10)

When I need guidance, he is my Wonderful Counselor. (See Isaiah 9:6)

When I need a loving Father, he is Abba Father—a very intimate relationship. (See Romans 8:15 and Galatians 4:6)

When I need comfort, he is the God of Comfort. (See 2 Corinthians 1:3–4)

When I need calming, he is my Prince of Peace. (See Isaiah 9:6)

When I need hope, he is my Risen Savior. (See Revelation 1:17–18)

3. God *Has* Blessed Us with Some Visible Revelations of Himself

More good news! One of my favorite passages is when Jesus revealed himself to John years after his death and resurrection (see Revelation 1:13–18). And later we're given a glorious glimpse of Heaven's Throne, where all are worshipping Holy God and the Lamb who was slaughtered (Jesus). (See Revelation: Chapters 4–5)

It's About Who God Is and His Relationship with Us

We *will* see him face to face, Scripture assures believers. But until then, it's good to remember that if we're preoccupied with how to envision him, or what we think we should feel, we miss *him*!

God has a unique and special relationship with each of us, and everyone's journey with him is different. We walk by faith. The more we seek him from the heart, and draw near to him, and hear his Word, the more he will reveal special glimpses of his glory to us in ways we would never imagine . . . or be able to explain to others.

Truly grateful for a faithful God who wants us to commune with him. Forever.

"Blessed *are* those who have not seen and *yet* have believed." ~Jesus (John 20:29b)

Will Your "Truth" Wash Away?

What I just love about my morning walks is talking with the Lord, delighting in all the amazing beauty, and praising him for his precious promises! Until last week. Ugh!

With colorful chalk and impeccable handwriting, someone had graced the sidewalk with the words of a poem about how we can all find peace *without God.* Just be kind, look around, and we'll find all we need right here, now. I wanted to cry. And throw up.

Overcome by grief, sadness, and anger, I was tempted to get my own chalk and write the *good* news about God's love and grace through Jesus Christ (the Prince of Peace), and how he has made a way for everyone to know him and his true peace forever!

Thankfully, my knee-jerk reaction transitioned into pondering and soul searching. After a long-life journey with the Lord through many deep dark valleys and glorious mountain tops, I know my relationship with him is real. And I wouldn't trade his Word, his love, his grace, his peace, or his joy for anything!

Yet I still struggled with how to put it all into one clear word picture I could communicate.

Every day I continued to walk on that sidewalk poem. And I smiled as I scuffed my feet, trying to assist the elements that were gradually washing the false words away. 😉

That's it! *The words are slowly washing away!* They will not hold up to time, or wear and tear. The temporarily beautiful chalk is fading away. Along with its false message.

I often wonder why people would not want God. And I think it has something to do with unwillingness to admit we are sinners and *need him*, resulting in a lifetime of pushing him away.

When our hearts become hardened toward God and his truth, we'll grasp at anything else that makes us feel good. And we choose to perceive it as truth. Or adopt a relative mindset, where whatever you want to believe becomes your truth.

The ultimate test is time. Will it "wash away?"

I love how Jesus said it: "Heaven and earth will pass away, but My words will by no means pass away" (Matthew 24:35).

Though I can't change other people, I can always be a channel of his love and kindness and truth and peace to all those he brings across my path. And the beauty is that we *will* find all we need forever in God, and God alone.

There is no greater peace, true joy, and solid hope.

Trust the Pilot

Taking off in a jet is always a thrill! Recently, as the plane was taxiing toward the runway, I was ready to go! But for some reason we stopped. And just sat there. Hmmm. And sat there. Grrrrrr.

I looked out my window and sure didn't see any reason why we weren't going. Getting quite impatient, I wanted to stand up and shout, "Okay! Anytime now! Hello?!"

Suddenly I saw a huge jet landing right in front of us! Hmmmm.

It occurred to me that the pilot knew something I didn't. He saw something I couldn't. Even though it seemed like he wasn't doing anything and there was no reason for the delay, I was *so* glad he waited!

When God doesn't instantly do what we ask, as humans who like to be in control, we quickly become frustrated. Next time I pray and there seems to be no answer, I want to remind myself:

God knows something I do not;
He sees something I do not; and
He is working even though I cannot see.

Life is filled with daunting uncertainties, from the thrill of a take-off to the dread of a "water landing" (euphemism for crashing into the ocean). The safest way to navigate through them all is to take God's advice:

Trust in the LORD with all your heart,
And lean not on your own understanding…
(Proverbs 3:5)

Faith is not necessarily feeling great all the time. It's often uncomfortable. And stretching. But it's this mysteriously intangible connection that draws us close to the Lord.

In the unknown.

It is leaning and relying on our Heavenly Pilot to get us safely where we need to go, and ultimately to our final destination: our Home in Heaven.

"Do not fear, little flock, for it is your Father's good pleasure to give you the kingdom." ~ Jesus (Luke 12:32)

Teeter-Totter of Trust

Remember teeter-totters, or seesaws? Did you ever get ejected while too high up, or worse—dropped with a thud from too high up? I discovered that the safest, most stable place on the teeter-totter is right in the center, where it never moves.

Whether it's our work, home life, social life, financial situation, health, hobbies, ministry, activities, etc., we all wobble. Why? Because our circumstances are always fluctuating!

I've been struggling lately with two extremes, kind of like a teeter-totter: pride and self-sufficiency on one end (being tempted to think I can do this on my own without God), and fear and anxiety on the other (being tempted to think the worst is going to happen and God won't be able to help).

I know we're supposed to trust the Lord, but *how do I keep from flying too high with pride and self-sufficiency, or bottoming out with fear and anxiety?*

If the safest place on a teeter-totter is in the center, the fulcrum, then that is where I want to be with God.

He never moves. His Word is my stability. My security. My freedom! Pride and fear only get worse the farther away from the center (him) I move, increasing the risk and danger.

Proverbs 3:5–6 says, **"Trust in the Lord with all your heart, And lean not on your own understanding."** No fear. No pride.

And Philippians 4:6 says, **"Be anxious for nothing, but in everything by prayer and supplication with thanksgiving, let your requests be made known to God. And the peace of God which surpasses understanding will guard your hearts and minds in Christ Jesus."** No fear. No pride.

So how do I trust God? I came up with the three Ts:

1. **Take** personally what he has promised to do.
2. **Talk** with him about what he has promised to do.
3. **Thank** him for what he has promised to do.

The more I do the three Ts, the closer to the center of the teeter-totter I am. Because *he is the center*, and that's where I belong!

Two Steps to Hope When Your Faith Doesn't Seem to Work

Ever feel like your faith isn't "working"? I've struggled along with everyone else with all the turbulence, violence, shortages, loss of life, and fears. Is our world running out of hope? It's easy to question, "Where is God in all this? And why isn't my faith working?"

When things and people you relied on for most of your life have seemingly collapsed beneath you, you wonder if it's safe to go to sleep at night or wake up in the morning. Many of us instinctively turn to God for answers, help, and hope. To fix it all!

And many others turn away from him in anger and resentment. How could I trust a God who allows pain, evil, injustice, and tragedy?

From the beginning, every generation has wrestled with these questions. Even those of us who seem to have a "strong faith." There are two things that have helped me recently: *taking a fresh look at faith, and then closely examining my own.*

1. What Is Faith?

A typical definition might be "Complete trust, confidence, or strong belief in someone or something." People say, "Just have more faith." But faith in and of itself has no value.

No matter how much faith I have in that bridge I cross, my only hope is in the bridge itself. Will it hold me up securely? Am I safe? I need to know it's the reliable way, that I can believe in it, and that my life will be safe as I cross. And even with just a teeny bit of faith, if the bridge is sturdy, it will support me as I travel safely and successfully to the other side.

Faith, a gift from God, is not a feeling that can be mustered up. It is action—taking steps based on who or what we believe.

The only value of faith is the reliability of its object.

2. Who and What Am I Trusting?

Many of us have grown up in a culture where we really felt little need to trust God for temporal things. For the most part, we had a stable government, decent economy, plenty of food, healthcare options, medicinal cures, jobs, retirement accounts, police protection, military protection, schools, travel, social events, and freedom.

By default, we have placed our faith in these weak, unreliable, and temporary things. Perhaps it's a blessing in disguise that we now see many of these broken bridges are not safe to cross.

Faith is not just wishful thinking. It is not placing our hope in what we think God is like, or what he should do for us. We must seek the truth he has revealed to us and place our trust in what he has said—what he has clearly promised.

Scripture shows us that our faith has value when it is placed in God and his Word:

" … Blessed *is* she who believed, for there will be a fulfillment of those things which were told her from the Lord." (Luke 1:45)

Nevertheless we, according to His promise, look for new heavens and a new earth in which righteousness dwells. (2 Peter 3:13)

Let us hold fast the confession of *our* hope without wavering, for He who promised *is* faithful. (Hebrews 10:23)

So if faith can't be contrived, where does it come from? Written from a prison cell while suffering for his faith, Paul wrote: "So then faith comes by hearing, and hearing by the word of God." (Romans 10:17).

The more we read God's Word, the more we will grow to know him, and learn what he promises. A good place to start is the gospel of John, the book of Romans, or Hebrews: Chapter 11.

When God—and what he has said—is the object of our faith, then and only then, do we have real hope.

Jesus said to him, "I am the way, the truth, and the life. No one comes to the Father except through Me." (John 14:6).

He Is the Bridge!

When we put all our faith in him, even if nothing changes around us, *we* will change. We will have a reason to be able to sleep at night and to get up in the morning.

And ultimately when our Savior takes us Home to Heaven, we will no longer need faith. For he is the beginner of it and the finisher of it, and the only one worthy of it! ♥

CHAPTER FIVE

Makes Ya Think

Prayer:

Thank YOU, Lord, for the gift of life. When its cares and distractions tug at me, please remind me of my final destination, and the abundant life you offer right now.

How Much Time Do You Have?

Remember when we were young (waaaay back there 😉), we assumed we'd have all the time in the world? In fact, time just couldn't move fast enough when Christmas was coming—or summer vacation, or our wedding, or our baby. Seems like it's a different story now. At least it was for Megan.

Several years ago, I invited Megan, a delightful young single mother, to our small group of neighbor ladies. I always closed the time together with a prayer. Sadly, she told me later that she really didn't want to come anymore because we were "too religious."

We still kept in touch, and remained friends. And when I was seriously ill, she offered to help…what a blessing! Megan and her daughter had a special place in my heart, and I prayed for them often.

Last year, Megan began her battle with cancer.

I rarely saw her after that, but continued to send her loving notes of encouragement, and cheery gifts via Amazon. I could tell when I'd walk past her house that things weren't going well.

A few weeks ago, her sister told me Megan was beginning hospice care that day, but there was no timeline. I went home and just wept. And prayed even more fervently for Megan and her family.

I gathered a gift basket for her, including a special note to Megan, and my book, *Goodbye for Now.* I hoped that she and her family could find some helpful, practical resources in it, to prepare for what was ahead, and to help after she passed. The book is also rich with comforting scriptures, a simple explanation of God's love for us, and an invitation to receive his gift of forgiveness and eternal life through Jesus Christ. I didn't expect to hear from her.

To my surprise, the next day on my front door, I found a sweet thank you note from Megan! She drew little hearts and expressed appreciation for all the love and kindness I'd shown her. And also that the book had already been a help, especially the practical parts. She ended with:

"I think the spiritual will come with time."

I was beyond elated! A window of hope! And I continued to pray even more.

Then I asked myself, *is she putting off getting right with God thinking she'll have plenty of time?*

I never heard from her again. Two weeks later she was gone.

It pains my heart every time I walk past her house. And I continue to pray for her family. I'll never know what took place between Megan and God in those final two weeks. But I'm so thankful that I was able to share the good news with her, and that she expressed some level of openness to it.

And yet I wonder . . . **how much time does each of us really have?**

The Lifeboat

Imagine for a moment that you were born and raised on the Titanic. You never had a choice as to your condition and destiny—that's just the way you began your existence in the universe. Having grown up quickly, you didn't mind this lifestyle. In fact, it was promising to be quite pleasurable.

You'd been taught that life has its ups and downs, its seasick moments, disappointments at the dinner table and on the dance floor. In fact, some people were angry at the captain, whom they'd never seen, questioning how he could allow pain and still claim to be a loving captain.

You'd also been taught the importance of being a good person in order to win the captain's favor and hopefully ensure a pleasant future.

Can You Trust the Ship?

You admired the beauty of the ship and reveled in its ability to provide you with the comforts of life you felt you deserved. You rested securely as you pondered the ship's strength. Alone with your thoughts, you were troubled momentarily by fleeting fear, which was quickly allayed as you drew comfort from what you saw around you. The truth was so evident—how could you have questioned it?

Chiding yourself for your moment of weakness, you reminded yourself that you could trust this ship—the ship you had grown to know and love, the ship that everyone knew was so solid and indestructible that there would never be a need for lifeboats.

Caught up in your immediate surroundings and the voyage itself, you neglected to notice the majesty of the roaring sea and the splendor of the star-studded sky at night. Who was responsible for all of that? **Had you considered your final destination?**

But why bother about those things? You were having a wonderful time in the present. There would be plenty of opportunities later to consider your destination.

Suddenly you were jolted awake by clamor and confusion. The ship was sinking. It was going down fast. Terrified, you cried, "Help! Help me!"

No one could help. They were going down too. The ship had failed you. All of your good deeds meant nothing for you now.

"Good news!" someone shouted. "It is finished! Everyone can now be saved!"

You learned that the captain himself had plunged into the black, icy water to release a giant lifeboat that floated to the surface. *They said that even before the ship was built the captain knew what he would have to do to provide the lifeboat.* You watched as the captain's body floated off into the darkness.

Freedom to Board

They said that the captain would never force anyone to get on the lifeboat, but that *he wanted the people to have the freedom to board willingly.* Amid the panic and confusion as the ship began to submerge, you observed this freedom of choice.

Some argued that it was pretty narrow thinking to claim there was only one lifeboat. Others clung to the ship, refusing to let go of their source of life and pleasure. Some sadly insisted that they weren't good enough to get into the lifeboat.

Others were indignant at the thought of boarding a lifeboat with imperfect people, hypocrites, and the politically incorrect. Realizing they had only minutes to live, some rushed to the dining room to eat all they could.

Politely, some granted you the right to believe in the lifeboat as long as you respected their right to believe differently. Others preferred to stick with their friends and family who had chosen to stay on the ship.

There were some who said the captain never died to provide a lifeboat. It was all *just a feel-good fairy tale giving everyone false hopes.*

Others were holding debates to prove that there never was a captain.

Some refused to listen, explaining that they knew all there was to know about lifeboats since they had gone to lifeboat class every Sunday. A few declined, complaining that they once tried to read the Lifeboat Instruction Manual but didn't understand it.

A few of the younger people weren't worried, since their parents were already aboard the lifeboat. Therefore, they too would be okay. Some said the captain was a good man but that he certainly was not capable of providing a lifeboat. *Others boasted that they didn't need a lifeboat as they began to swim to shore.*

Some expressed offense at the scare tactics, getting people all upset when there wasn't a problem. *The ship was fine, they claimed.* Still others argued cynically that the lifeboat was just a moneymaking scheme.

Talk of other lifeboat options distracted many from boarding the real lifeboat. Some were determined to complain about the captain for allowing discomfort and refused to accept that he really cared.

Calmly, others said that *there was still plenty of time.* They would get into the lifeboat after they had had a chance to live their lives. Some challenged the belief that a safe shore even existed, since, like the captain, the shore could not be seen.

Still others complained that the lifeboat was all they ever heard about, and they wished certain people would quit shoving lifeboat information down their throats.

And a few reached out and climbed to safety in the lifeboat.

What would you do?

Now is a good time to decide. The captain is waiting on the shore for you with open arms.

Secure Your Place in the Lifeboat

How do we secure our places in the lifeboat? Salvation, our lifeboat, comes only through Christ's death—the death of the Captain who rose again and is now waiting for us. Here are the steps he gives us to securing our salvation.

1. *Acknowledge your desperate need, and helplessness as a sinner before God.* "…for all have sinned and fall short of the glory of God… " (Romans 3:23).

2. *Believe that God loves you and Christ died for you.* "But God demonstrates His own love toward us, in that while we were still sinners, Christ died for us" (Romans 5:8).

3. *Realize there is nothing you can do to earn salvation. By faith we must receive God's free gift of eternal life through his Son.* "For the wages of sin *is* death, but the gift of God *is* eternal life in Christ Jesus our Lord" (Romans 6:23).

4. *Honestly admit to God that you need him.* "For 'whoever calls on the name of the LORD shall be saved'" (Romans 10:13).

5. *Trust him to carry you safely to shore.*

> He who has the Son has life; he who does not have the Son of God does not have life. These things I have written to you who believe in the name of the Son of God, that you may know that you have eternal life, and that you may *continue to* believe in the name of the Son of God. (1 John 5:12–13)

And that is real HOPE! ♥

****

~Excerpt from my book, *Goodbye for Now*

Praise the Tree?

On a recent morning walk to the woods, enraptured in a dazzling moment of joy, I paused to lift up my hands in worship. My moment ended abruptly as someone mockingly called out, "Praise the tree!"

Smiling, I responded, "I'm praising the *Creator of the tree.*" She immediately shifted the conversation to the weather. 😉

Saddened that she couldn't share my joy of communing with the Lord of creation, I got to thinking about what it would be like if we had no Creator. If all we had was the tree.

It seems so unnatural, distorted and bizarre, that many humans have chosen throughout history to worship the created thing—rather than the Creator. The Bible explains that all men have been given the opportunity to glorify God as our Creator.

But once we start hardening our hearts and refusing to worship God, he gradually lets go. *What a frightening thought*!

It's my guess that when we reject God and choose to offer our devotion to something immensely inferior, the reward is either an adrenaline high, or perhaps a false feeling of having done something "good." There is also no obligation to repent of sin, and no threat of an interpersonal relationship.

The tragedy is that the counterfeit blinds us to the glory of the truth.

We live in a time where worship of the creation and not the Creator is clearly becoming the popular choice. I'm so thankful that in spite of our bent to rebel against God, in love and grace, *he still came down from Heaven to heal our broken relationship with him.*

The good news is that when we take that first step toward him, to seek him as our Creator and Savior Jesus Christ, the desire to know him and worship him just keeps growing.

I encourage you to look today for his love messages to you through his creation and his written Word. Not only can we have a personal relationship with the God of the universe forever, we can also deeply enjoy his glorious creation now, and ultimately in the new Heaven and Earth.

There is nothing that could ever compare to knowing and worshipping God!

Praise God!

Two Mistakes People Make Before They Die

Many mistakes are reparable. These two aren't. The irony is that everyone has the luxury of avoiding these disasters, but unfortunately those who get it right are the exception.

A good friend of mine recently died suddenly, leaving his son to wade through the tangled mess he left behind. An outdated will was the least of the debacle. Doing his best just to function amid the waves of grief, his son had no clue about any of his accounts or passwords, and was overwhelmed with all the unfinished business and loose ends.

How much smoother things would have gone had he taken the time to get things organized, and then communicated with his son where he could find the information.

The first big mistake we can make is to *not* put our earthly affairs in order.

In my book, *Goodbye for Now: Practical Help and Personal Hope for Those Who Grieve,* a section is devoted to preparing for our own "goodbye." One of the items on the list is to clean out clutter. As I was sharing this with a group, one older fellow boasted, "I'm not doing that. It's my revenge!" Still chuckling at that, but it actually will make a big difference for those who are left behind if we do all we can in advance to put things in order.

The awkwardness and unpleasantness of discussing our desires, decisions, and information with our loved ones pales in comparison to how it will feel later for them if we don't.

A few other ideas included in the book are:

___ Collect and organize all pertinent info.
___ Be sure your will or trust is legal and up to date.
___ Complete an advance directive.
___ Put all your important information in an obvious or agreed-upon place.
___ Pay your debts.
___ Consider being a donor, either organ and tissue or whole body.
___ Examine the options for prepaid funeral home services.
___ Write out what you want in your service.
___ Attend to any rifts with family or friends.
___ Be at peace with God.

We all have many opportunities to make our peace with God by receiving his free gift of salvation through Jesus Christ his Son. It is eternally tragic to reject God's loving offer!

The second and by far biggest mistake we can make this side of Heaven is to *not* put our heavenly affairs in order.

The clamor of daily life is such a powerful distraction that we can easily assume there will be ample time to take care of things *later*. But we all know that any of us could go at any time. Don't wait until you're sick, and don't wait until you're older.

Why not enjoy today and everyday from now on, knowing *whose we are, and where we are going*? I hope you can take the time to pause and be sure you are ready. ♥

When both our earthly affairs and our heavenly affairs are in order, not only do *we* have peace of mind and heart, but we also spare our loved ones added burdens to their grief.

The good news is that if you are reading this, you still have time to do it right!

Island Sun

"I would love to be lying on a tropical beach right now! I deserve to be lying on a tropical beach right now. Oh that's just great. It's raining!"

Sound familiar? Most of us struggle every day with discontentment in spite of the fact that the Lord tells us to be content.

So just what is at the heart of our frustrations? (Other than the basic fact that we *should* be lying on an island beach soaking up the sun, sipping a cool drink, munching on chips and candy bars to our heart's content… all without sunburn, indigestion, or weight gain.)

Or perhaps more realistically, we long for a Godly soul mate, or a fulfilling job (or a job at all), or a nice home, or relief from a difficult health condition. These seem like reasonable desires.

At what point do my natural longings become unhealthy discontentment?

I came up with three questions to ask myself when I start to complain:

1. Am I worshipping a sovereign God, or one of my own making? Do I truly embrace the fact that my God can do anything, and he has a loving wise plan for me? Or do I cling to the Santa Claus-in-the-sky fantasy of a God who should give me everything I want?

2. Am I living for present temporary pleasure, or true lasting eternal treasure? Will what I desire hold its value over time and forever, or am I seeking to always feel good regardless of the future?

3. Am I demanding entitlements, or am I cherishing gifts? We were born demanding everything, and some of us have never outgrown it. Since most of us have grown up with plenty, it's hard to accept that we do not deserve a decent car, hot showers, unlimited food, or a pain-free body.

Continuous comfort is too often our goal. We like these things, but they're blessings to appreciate, not entitlements to demand.

Hebrews 13:5 encourages us along these same lines:

"*Let your* conduct *be* without covetousness; *be* content with such things as you have. For He Himself has said, 'I will never leave you nor forsake you.'"

It's easier to be content when I remember that my *God is sovereign and is with me, that he has an endless plan in action for my good,* and therefore I choose to give thanks for all he is and all his blessings. And as I do, the day already seems a little warmer and brighter! 

Which Way, Lord?

Ever had the thrill of riding in bumper cars at an amusement park? And live to tell about it?

Whee! It was supposed to be fun, but as a little kid, unfortunately, I was everyone's favorite target. Slammed! Bombarded! Helpless and alone, it was anything but fun. And I didn't know how to find my way out of the middle of the mess.

Eventually when I was tall enough, I got to drive the little race cars on a guided track. Now that was fun! And I didn't have to steer perfectly. Sure I wobbled a bit, but the track kept me going in the right direction. I felt safe.

Funny how life has turned out to have its share of bumper-car moments, when we are feeling slammed, overwhelmed, and in need of protection and direction.

Making choices can be daunting. And life continuously bombards us with challenges where we need to know which way to go. Wouldn't it be nice to have a guided track?

Oh, wait… we do! Psalm 16:11 reminds us that the Lord will direct us, and will be with us…and tops it off with joy!

You will show me the path of life;
In Your presence *is* fullness of joy;
At Your right hand *are* pleasures forevermore.
(Psalm 16:11)

So when those bumper-car moments slam us, we can choose to trust him. When we know the Lord, we are on a guided track, with him. Even if we can't see very far ahead.

And it's okay if we don't steer perfectly. 🙂

CHAPTER SIX

Surprises

Prayer:

Thank you, Lord, that nothing is ever a surprise to you. Please help us trust you to always give us what we need when we need it.

Poinsettia Plot Twist

I love when you start the day with grand plans, and then the Lord surprises you with the unexpected! Wanting to brighten someone's day with a beautiful poinsettia, my day began with asking God to show me who needed it.

Immediately, I was excited to take it to the nearby care facility and ask them who could use a special visit. Praying for the Lord's leading and blessing, and especially for the individual I'd soon meet, I just wanted to share his love.

Plot Twist #1:

The staff were so appreciative! They said most of the residents do not get visitors. However they wanted the poinsettia to be placed in the big room so everyone could enjoy it. Okay… I get that.

With no poinsettia to give, I still wanted to know who could use a little love and cheer. Lighting up, the nurse led me down the hall and introduced me to Rebecca, a very special lady on hospice, who was also blind. (She could never have seen the poinsettia!) I was so excited to be able to share the love of Jesus with her, and the hope and peace he offers.

Plot Twist #2:

I held Rebecca's hand as we chatted about Christmas. In a matter of minutes, we discovered we were both believers! So much joy. An instant bond.

Plot Twist #3:

My original plan to stay a few minutes blossomed into a beautiful visit between two people sharing love and joy and thankfulness, in spite of the pain and hardships of this life. Then she quietly said to me, "My name isn't Rebecca. It's Pam."

I couldn't stop laughing, and I asked her if we needed to start all over. She was all smiles!

Plot Twist #4:

Our time together was so sweet. Before I left, I prayed with her and gave her a long warm hug.

Then she said to me, "I am so lonely, and this morning I prayed that the Lord would send someone to visit with me."

WOW. ♥

The biggest plot twist was that I went to *be* a blessing, and I *received* one instead.

Never underestimate the significance of asking the Lord to direct your path.

And never underestimate your potential to touch lives with his love. ♥

> **" ... And the King will answer and say to them, 'Assuredly, I say to you, inasmuch as you did it to one of the least of these My brethren, you did it to Me.' . . . "**
> (Matthew 25:40)

The Richest Reunions: Looking Backward or Forward?

Summer is a popular time for reunions, whether for family, school, military, or other common bonds. We have already attended several, and more are on the schedule. But what I experienced last week truly woke me up, and I will never again look at reunions in the same way.

Sizzling barbecued burgers, laughter, and lots of hugs are part of the leisurely time of reconnecting and reminiscing with those with whom we share common bonds. We talk about those who are no longer with us, tell stories and share memories, and often discover things we had not previously known. These reunions are a time of mixed emotions based on the past. *We are looking backward.*

Then there is a different kind of reunion. Last week, I was honored to participate in the memorial service for a dear friend. Through teary eyes we reflected on her life, well lived for the Lord, and we also looked ahead at her future with him forever. In spite of our sadness in missing her, it was such a joy to celebrate her new life and to reconnect with people we had not seen in years. It was a joy that made me almost feel guilty.

Then it hit me: the deep true joy of this reunion was future focused!

And these bonds far exceed mere earthly limitations. When all we have is the earthbound tie of the past, there is something missing—hope. Truthfully, it can be depressing.

But when we are able to look forward, based on the promises of our God who never lies and our paid debt on the cross by our Savior, our souls are touched and united with true peace. And joy!

In these future-focused reunions, reflecting on our past as believers confirms that there has been—and will be—a purpose for it all. And knowing it will be our own memorial service at some point motivates us to seek the Lord and his truth and life even more fervently.

And for me, the greatest motivation is knowing that the ultimate reunion in Heaven is the one I do not want to miss!

". . . that in the dispensation of the fullness of the times He might gather together in one all things in Christ, both which are in heaven and which are on earth—in Him." (Ephesians 1:10)

Mold-Hound Surprise

Several years ago, I was fighting for my life. I had to force food down, was nauseated and bloated, had panic awakenings all night, was weak and could barely function. Terrified to go to sleep and to wake up, I just wanted to quit. My doctors were baffled and doubted I'd make it. Only the Lord and the prayers of many kept me going.

Finally, a new doctor found the problem: severe mold toxicity!

I found a place to stay for the summer while the house we loved was turned upside down in remediation. We lost almost everything. I'm so grateful for my amazing husband who cared for me and also oversaw the entire demolition and reconstruction.

Six months later I was starting to feel better. It's been a slow process, and I'll probably always struggle with the challenges of post-traumatic stress.

Still, my gratitude continues to outshine the darkness.

While I continued to get stronger and our life returned to normal, one mystery remained: no active source of mold was ever found.

One day my doctor recommended the house be tested again, just to be on the safe side. Panic gripped me! I felt like throwing up and running away. I could *never* go through that again!

But after much prayer, we decided to go ahead.

We enlisted the help of a company recommended by my doctor. Their young Beagle, Jax, was professionally trained to locate mold. Jax's owners had lost their home and health to mold illness too, leading to their dedication to help others.

Finally, inspection day arrived. The suspense was intense. Would we soon be grieving the loss of our home and belongings again, or celebrating a healthy home?

When Jax came in, he rested his head on my lap while I stroked his soft ears and talked dog to him. It was an amazing, much-needed dose of comfort.

Jax's owner explained the procedure and invited us to observe. Signaling that it was time to work, he commanded, "Jax, seek!" He led him around the room on a loose leash while Jax sniffed away.

Suddenly Jax sat, alerting to mold. Bummer!

Jax pointed his nose up toward a specific spot. He was rewarded with praise and a treat, and that spot was marked with blue tape.

As fascinating as it was, I couldn't bear to watch anymore. So I went out for a long walk. And prayed!

When I returned, there were pieces of blue tape in *every* room! *Not good.*

The owner then walked us through the house, noting that most of the blue tape was far from any water source, with no visible mold nearby. Then it dawned: each spot was in the path of a furnace vent. This led us downstairs to the HVAC closet.

There we saw two more pieces of tape on a corner brick wall. Still no visible mold or moisture. He climbed into the furnace closet and pointed inside, way in back. And there it was! Down below where no one had ever looked, or even considered looking, right behind the brick wall.

Good boy, Jax! 👍

We heaved a sigh of relief. It all made sense! All the spots could be traced to mold in the HVAC closet — which was scary-ugly.

I wanted to invite Jax to live with us, but we had to say goodbye.

The blessings continued. The HVAC and mold remediation teams were able to come right away, and within a few days the mold was successfully removed. We were thanking the Lord and rejoicing!

Our journey isn't over. The mystery of how and where the water came in remains to be solved. So, we will watch and wait. And continue to trust the Lord, Jehovah-Jireh, Our Provider, who takes care of us *in* the hard times.

And nothing ever surprises him.

For now, I'm going to turn on the furnace, and thank the Lord for the privilege of living in a healthy home.

Our Hearing Can Improve

"Good news: Our hearing can improve as we get older."

"What?"

"I SAID, OUR HEARING CAN IMPROVE AS WE GET OLDER!"

"Oh, good. How?"

Glad you asked. 🙂 Pondering this lately, I asked myself two questions:

1) *How does God speak to me?* And 2) *What gets in the way of me hearing him?*

A few weeks ago I flopped down very frustrated, pouring out my complaint to the Lord, and "prayed" (a.k.a. politely told him what I wanted him to do). Suddenly it occurred to me: Have I paused to ask, "Lord, what do you want?" It was a stark and humbling realization that I had not been listening, nor had I even consciously considered it.

Now thanks to a yellow sticky note on my desk, I am regularly reminded to ask him what he wants . . . and to listen. I am still a work in progress, but my moments of being consciously receptive to God are becoming delightfully more frequent.

Here are three things that are helping:

1. Dealing with the stuff that gets in the way of me truly **wanting to hear God.** Do I need to check my priorities? My attitude? Inventory my relationships?

2. Making the time and **taking the time to hear** what God has already been speaking to us for thousands of years . . . through my Bible, a treasure just sitting on the shelf like an unopened gift.

3. Pushing "pause" on my perpetually preoccupied mind, and reprograming it to be more **consciously receptive**

to God throughout the day and night—both my mind and my heart.

At the end of each day, I want to reflect on all the surprising ways God spoke to me. (And I actually heard.)

Maybe through a hug, a song, a sunset, a tree, a kind word, a flower, fresh air, a social media post, singing birds, a disappointment, a pet, laughter, a storm, a promise from his Word, an answer to prayer, etc. God speaks to each of us uniquely—in a special way, and what a joy to start having little private "pinholes to Heaven," as I call them.

The good news is that it is possible for our hearing to improve. But first we need to *choose to listen.*

"Be still, and know that I *am* God." (Psalm 46:10a)

Good News, Bad News

(Content warning: This story may be difficult for those who have experienced trauma, pain, or loss related to pregnancy, childbirth, or parenting.)

Remember how funny those "good news, bad news" jokes used to be? I do! But this time it was not a joke.

When my son and daughter-in-law enthusiastically announced to us that they were expecting a baby, of course I cried. (Isn't that what prospective grandmas do?) We were all so very excited!

It was all I could do to not go shopping right then and there, and not stock up on necessary (or unnecessary) baby paraphernalia for our home. All in due time…

A few months later my son called. "Mom, I have good news and bad news," he began. Not at all braced for what was coming, I replied lightheartedly, "Okay…good news first."

"Well," he announced, "we're having a girl." My heart leaped with joy! The girl I never had. What a blessing! "But," he went on—interrupting my bliss—"the doctor said she may be brain dead."

Not sure what else took place after that. I was stunned. In shock.

After hanging up the phone I flung myself on the bed. I wept. I wailed. And I cried out to God. "Please! Why have you allowed this? Please! Save that precious little girl!"

The next several weeks dragged on. I wrestled with God. Begged. Pleaded. I was angry at this cruel injustice! I grieved for this priceless unborn baby. The pain of my loss and our loss as a family was insurmountable. Yet my husband and I prayed fervently. We prayed together as a family. Nonstop. We did not give up.

I don't know why God allows some things, and at other times he intervenes.

Why pain and grief for some, and healing and life for others? All I know is that I believe he does love us, and he is good. And *he is fully capable of giving us everything we need when we need it.*

So as I grieved, my prayer was eventually changed. I finally came to the point of letting go. True release. Now instead of just, "God fix this!" my heart honestly cried, "Please heal her. And if you do not, please give us all we need to love her and care for her in the best way we can."

As little Katherine continued to grow in the womb, we persisted in prayer, not knowing who we would welcome into this world, or if we even would. Keenly aware of my own agony, I cannot even imagine the pain and torment her own mother and father endured. But they faithfully held on to their God, and took it one day at a time.

Finally, with increased fervency in our prayers, the highly anticipated due date arrived. As a high-risk pregnancy from the beginning, they were all set up in the best possible medical center for the birth. What news would we receive when the phone rang? I fought off the temptation to rehearse all the possible scenarios.

After over forty hours of horrendously intense labor, we got the call. This was it! Katherine was born. That was the good news! Great news! A miracle in itself! And mother was doing well. Another miracle.

Then the other news came. The long-awaited news.

And believe it or not—it was also good. She was fine! Is there such a thing as good shock? I cautiously dared to really believe it. Squealing with exuberance, I threw my arms around my husband and shouted, **"Thank you!"** to God.

Curiously, the doctors were not sure why she was doing so well, and why the brain abnormality was now totally normal. Hmmm. (I have a pretty good idea.)

When she was just hours old, I wept as I held her for the first time.

Looking into her eyes, I whispered tenderly, "Katherine, we have been praying for you for a long time. We're so glad you are here. *Jesus loves you.*" And she cooed. (Seriously . . . I have witnesses!)

I instructed my son to never ever forget that she is a miracle baby. And if she receives a "bad" report card, puts a dent in the car, or brings home a weird boyfriend, to remember this day.

I still do not know why God sometimes says, "Yes," and sometimes, "No." Why life is filled with both good news and bad news.

But I choose to trust him no matter what he deems best.

And every time I hold that little girl on my lap, or look into her grown up eyes someday, I will never forget that she is a miracle. And I will always remind her that Jesus loves her. *And that is always good news!*

A New View

"Great Scott! Are you serious? Pretty sure the mirror is broken, because this looks like me in forty years!" Ah... the side effects of cataract surgery they forgot to mention.

Eventually pulling myself together after that reverse-Photoshop awakening, I was flooded with a gamut of delightful surprises. Tears welled up as I marveled at being able to distinguish the tiny sprouts of new growth on the tips of the cedars—and later, the actual rain drops in a refreshing downpour.

Then suddenly out of nowhere appeared little splotches of food in lovely places like the cabinets, walls, and floor. The best surprise was when I found that glob of toothpaste that had fallen off my toothbrush a few nights before. Looks like I have my work cut out for me from here on!

Sitting now without my glasses, I'm reminded of the prayer "God grant me the serenity to accept the things I cannot change, the courage to change the things I can, and the wisdom to know the difference." The more we trust the Lord and his goodness, the more fulfilling the journey is with him.

Whatever our challenges and changes may be, we choose how we respond.

As I continue on in this new chapter of life, I'm less likely to be critical of how someone or their house looks. I'm less likely to walk past a blooming flower without reveling in its beauty. And I'm more likely to be grateful every day for the privilege of appreciating our many blessings—past, present and future.

And is it my imagination, or is the food tastier, the songbirds sweeter, and the air fresher? (The drugs have worn off by now, so it's not that.) I think when we're willing to embrace something new and beautiful, we discover the beauty has been there all along.

Now it's up to us to choose to see it. 

Oh, taste and see that the LORD is good;
Blessed *is* the man *who* trusts in Him!
(Psalm 34:8)

Blessings

Prayer:

Thank you, Lord, for your mercy and lovingkindness, poured out before we were born and promised forever. Please open our hearts to joyfully receive all you have for us.

I Want Real Blessings!

Ever read a scripture promise and don't admit that you aren't really all that excited about it? I do. (Shock!) I'm thinking about the verse that says, "Blessed *be* the God and Father of our Lord Jesus Christ, who has blessed us with every spiritual blessing in the heavenly *places* in Christ . . ." (Ephesians 1:3).

When I first read that years ago, *I thought, I don't want spiritual blessings. I want* **real** *blessings!*

I wanted a horse, a boyfriend, and to look good in a bikini. As I got a little older, I wanted a car, a husband, and to look good in shorts. A few years later, I wanted a house, a baby, and to be able to fit into my jeans. And so it went. . . .

Now years later, I look back and most of those "real" blessings are gone (except the baby who is *really big* now). They were good at the time, but only temporary. Hmmm. They are no longer "real."

Perhaps that's why spiritual blessings are to be valued. Sought after. Cherished! Because only what is permanent is ultimately real.

Only what is permanent is ultimately real.

Some of those "spiritual blessings" offered in Ephesians 1 are:

*Forgiveness of sins. (Permanent. *Real.*)
*Accepted in the Beloved. (Permanent. *Real.*)
*Adopted as sons of God. (Permanent. *Real.*)
*Obtained an inheritance. (Permanent. *Real.*)
*Sealed by the Holy Spirit of promise. (Permanent. *Real.*)

Ultimately, all blessings come from God. And I'm truly grateful for even those that have not lasted.

But the best ones are those that are permanent . . . because they are the only real blessings. I guess that is because God is permanent. And He is real.

Now I am excited!

Treasures In the Valley of Pain

(Several years ago, I wrote this while still *in* the deep valley.)

For the past year, I've been struggling with several serious health issues, including one which affected my ability to eat for many months, and others which have been affecting my ability to sleep at night and function during the day. Needless to say, being in survival mode for so long has truly taken its toll on me.

Not sure where I'd be right now if it weren't for the Lord, and my wonderful husband, and the many dear people who have been praying. I kept dreaming of the day when I could write about how I was all recovered, and then I could rejoice with everyone! I kept waiting until I was all well and had something I could share.

Today with puffy eyes and tear drenched cheeks, I realize I don't have to wait. I need to write while I am still *in* the valley. As I started writing down what I have been learning, I was overwhelmed with how much the Lord *has* been doing in my life. I've learned and grown so much, even if it doesn't feel like it.

I share with you while I am *in my struggle* on this journey, to encourage anyone else who may be going through a really tough time.

If we stay open to the Lord, there are always treasures in the valley, no matter how dark or deep.

- ♥ *I am always safe because Jesus is always with me.*
- ♥ *The more I let go of what I assumed I'm entitled to, the freer I am.*
- ♥ *Don't wait until I feel great and my circumstances are ideal to love the Lord, and seek him, and trust him with all my heart.*
- ♥ *Thank the Lord for everything as if it had been taken away and then given back.*
- ♥ *Look for the pinholes to Heaven, God's love messages.*
- ♥ *Let the tears, trauma, and other emotions flow out freely.*
- ♥ *Deeply receive all the love and prayers from others who care.*
- ♥ *The more I smile and do joyful things like sing and dance, the better I will feel. Emotions follow motion.*
- ♥ *Be still (stop striving to figure it all out and fix it), and know that he is God.*
- ♥ *Sometimes God calls us to rest for a season; give myself permission to rest.*
- ♥ *Keep all my senses open to his blessings.*
- ♥ *All I need to do is trust God right now, for right now.*
- ♥ *Celebrate even the tiniest signs of progress, rather than focus on how far I still have to go.*
- ♥ *Sitting at Jesus's feet and listening to Him has immeasurable present and eternal value.*
- ♥ *Take steps to do what is good for me even if it is hard.*
- ♥ *Accept the fact that the older we get, the more we will have to release.*
- ♥ *Offer love, kindness, and encouragement to others along the way. You never know who else may be hurting too.*
- ♥ *Remember the cross and our risen Savior, and be assured the best is yet to come.*

- ♥ *Ask myself if it would make any difference if I could actually see Jesus with me?*
- ♥ *Filter down to what is absolutely essential for me to do, and set aside what can wait or have someone else help.*
- ♥ *The more I think about him and immerse myself in his Word, the more peace he gives me.*
- ♥ *Am I willing to pray for others in the way that I desperately need them to pray for me?*
- ♥ *Before going to sleep at night, focus on one beautiful moment of the day, and thank the Lord.*
- ♥ *I choose my thoughts, and by his Spirit my mind can be filled with hope and peace, rather than dwelling on what I wish were different.*
- ♥ *Rejoice in the Lord and his precious promises, even if I don't feel like it. Eternity is on the schedule, even if it seems like I'll never make it through the day or night or hour or moment.*

Jesus himself is the ultimate treasure. He will either carry me safely through, or carry me safely Home. Or both. ♥

Wardrobe Wishlist

I *love* new clothes! It's dangerously easy to buy whatever we want these days. And have it delivered before we've time to walk to the front porch!

I tried on a pair of last year's shorts and was so discouraged. They just didn't fit anymore. Ready to browse online for a new pair, I realized I had them on backward!

Then there are socks. I have friends who don't care if they match. Not sure I'll ever be that liberated, but good for them. So assuming I was ready for more socks, I tackled the sock drawer. (Just getting it open was a victory). Much to my surprise and delight, I found socks galore—some still brand new—with plenty to toss or give away. And the icing on the cake was a wad of cash I stashed away years ago!

No need for new shorts. No need for new socks. Surely there was something I needed! I know . . . new hangers. You always need hangers, right?

Well, once I hit the closet, I found a bunch of stuff I could give away, and guess what? I have hangers now!

So it looks like the anticipated shopping spree is on hold for now. Pretty sure it won't take long for me to think of other things I need.

Or maybe, perhaps, I'm discovering that I don't need as much as I thought. And actually *have* more than I realized.

I wonder if acquiring things can become more important than giving thanks.

Something to think about. We have so many blessings! And what a joy when we can appreciate them, and the one who blesses us.

Going to go enjoy today, with my shorts that fit, and my socks that match.

(I am, however, on the lookout for toothpaste-colored shirts.)

Praise the Lord!
Oh, give thanks to the Lord, for He is good!
For His mercy endures forever.
(Psalm 106:1)

Our Forever Helper—Guaranteed!

Just when you think you're getting close to knowing it all (haha 😆) someone asks a monumental question: "Who is the Holy Spirit, what does he do, and does it matter to me?" Hmmmm. Wow.

After weeks of seeking the Lord's help and digging through scripture, what a blessing to discover many amazing truths about the mysterious Holy Spirit!

Who is he?

The Bible reveals that the Holy Spirit is a "person," not an impersonal force. He displays intellect, emotions, and will. He is deity, coequal with the Father and the Son.

And it's okay if we can't totally grasp this. (If you're scratching your head, that's normal.) It's good to realize there's so much about God that remains a mystery for now.

What does he do?

The Holy Spirit convicts us of sin (makes us keenly aware of our desperate need for a Savior) and opens our spiritual eyes to see the truth of the Gospel. He gives us faith to believe.

Those who respond to this conviction, and by faith choose to believe in Jesus Christ, receive eternal life and a new spiritual nature.

He is our Helper. Literally, he comes alongside.

Jesus promised, "And I will pray the Father, and He will give you another Helper, that He may abide with you forever—the Spirit of truth . . . " (John 14:16–17a).

He is our Advocate, Comforter, Encourager, and Counselor.

The Holy Spirit gives every believer spiritual gifts—abilities for service. What a blessing to be part of God's master plan!

He prays for us. ♥

The Holy Spirit guides us into truth, and glorifies Jesus.

He works in us and through us.

When we give ourselves fully to him, the Spirit produces the supernatural "fruit of the Spirit."

"But the fruit of the Spirit is love, joy, peace, longsuffering, kindness, goodness, faithfulness, gentleness, self-control." (Galatians 5:22-23a)

He brings to mind thoughts of God and hunger for his Word, and prompts us to seek him and pray.

The Holy Spirit indwells the believer permanently. He secures our future!

The Holy Spirit seals the believer. A seal denotes something that is officially notarized. The Holy Spirit is our spiritual heavenly birth certificate.

He is our pledge—our guarantee from God, **"who also has sealed us and given us the Spirit in our hearts as a guarantee"** (2 Corinthians 1:22).

And one day, he will give eternal spiritual life to our mortal bodies. Hallelujah!

Does it matter?

It matters only if you truly want:

- Spiritual eyes opened and faith to believe;
- Eternal life and a new spiritual nature;
- A forever Helper to come alongside;

- An Advocate, Comforter, Encourager, and Counselor;
- Spiritual gifts for service as part of God's master plan;
- To be prayed for in heavenly realms;
- To be guided into Truth;
- God to work in you and through you;
- Supernatural love, joy, peace, longsuffering, kindness, goodness, faithfulness, gentleness, and self-control (see Galatians 5:22–23)
- Thoughts of God and hunger for his Word;
- An eternally secure future;
- A new forever body.

I hope it matters to you. There's no one better to trust today, and forever!

> **In Him you also *trusted,* after you heard the word of truth, the gospel of your salvation; in whom also, having believed, you were sealed with the Holy Spirit of promise, who is the guarantee of our inheritance until the redemption of the purchased possession, to the praise of His glory.** (Ephesians 1:13–14)

~~~~~~~~~~~~

For additional input, I encourage you to use a concordance to explore the wealth of amazing scriptures about the Holy Spirit.

~~~~~~~~~~~~

The Hungry Woodpecker

"What's that awful noise?!?" Peering down the street I saw a woodpecker pecking its heart out on a metal chimney cover. Yikes!

Annoyed but not too worried, I figured he'd soon realize the futility of his fruitless folly and move on to more satisfying cuisine.

Oops… I was wrong. This bird was very determined! Not sure what the payoff was, but he stuck with it for a long time.

The next day on my walk, there he was again—pecking away more fervently than ever. Scratching my head, I was baffled. Maybe this was a mating call of some kind. Even so, he would eventually have to eat.

My initial amusement soon turned to sadness. My heart felt heavy. *Doesn't he know he's not going to get any food from that metal cap? And how long will he keep trying until he realizes it? Or will he just peck harder?*

Then I started thinking about us as humans. I wonder what the birds think when they observe people pouring all we have into something that will never permanently satisfy our deepest needs. And yet we just keep pecking and pecking.

I'm guessing there must be some kind of immediate payoff, but even that is temporary at best.

My heart grieves for the prostitute on the corner, the addict, the compulsive spender deeply in debt, and the one looking for love in all the wrong places. **But perhaps even more for the person who looks fine on the outside but has chosen to fill the emptiness with anything other than God.**

Not sure where I'd be today if it weren't for the grace of God through Jesus. I, too, was searching for deep and lasting soul satisfaction in so many dead-ends.

I have heard it said: *"The only one who can satisfy the human heart is the one who made it."* And I have found this to be true. 

Oh how I wish I could tell that hungry woodpecker that there's a lush forest nearby able to satisfy him beyond his wildest dreams!

For He satisfies the longing soul,
And fills the hungry soul with goodness.
(Psalm 107:9)

A Continual Feast

Have you ever had a food fantasy? My favorite is a free all-you-can-eat buffet. 24/7. And with no consequences! 😆

I was born hungry, and for years I thought I was the only one who loved eating more than anything else. How ironic that most of my life I've dealt with food-related challenges: health, dental, digestive, weight, emotional, etc. But bittersweet because the hard times just make me even more grateful for the blessing of eating good food.

Today I came across a verse that jumped right off the page:

. . . he who is of a merry heart *has* a continual feast.
(Proverbs 15:15b)

Wow! Sounds good to me! As much as we all enjoy eating, there's something far greater and more deeply satisfying than the temporary pleasure food brings.

It's free, and it keeps going on and on! But just how do we get a merry heart? Especially in today's world.

For me, joy, happiness and a merry heart result from the choices we make. Our wise Creator has so lovingly formed our brains, bodies, and emotions to harvest the fruit of happiness from consistently sowing his seeds of hope. There are things we can do to grow our joy.

Here's what is helping me:

1. Choose to trust him. "And whoever trusts in the Lord, happy *is* he" (Proverbs 16:20b). A merry heart results from us taking those steps of faith, trusting who God is and what He has said.

2. Choose to rejoice in him. Regardless of our circumstances we can always rejoice in our Savior! "Yet I will rejoice in the Lord, I will joy in the God of my salvation" (Habakkuk 3:18).

3. Choose merry actions. Give thanks, sing songs of praise, laugh, dance, make silly faces, smile! "Is anyone cheerful? Let him sing psalms" (James 5:13b). The more we actively live in joy, the more we will feel it. A great thing I learned from my counselor is that "emotion follows motion." Sometimes we have to *do* before we can *feel.*

The more we feed on these uplifting things, the merrier our hearts. And the merrier our hearts, the more we'll find ourselves doing these things! Isn't God good?

And before you know it, the feast begins.

Trust in the Lord, and do good;
Dwell in the land, and feed on His faithfulness.
Delight yourself also in the Lord,
And He shall give you the desires of your heart.
(Psalm 37:3-4)

Changing Seasons: A New Take

It seems like I've spent most of my life either waiting for summer to come, or wishing it were still here. Why can't it always be summertime? As a kid, going back to school was scary, and as a teacher it was downright frightening!

Feeling the chill of impending winter got me down again this year. Moping around in woe-is-me mode, it suddenly hit me!

***He* changes the times and the seasons.** (Daniel 2:21a)

Well, we all pretty much know that, but do we really get it? I didn't. Until now. When I find myself complaining about what is out of my control, and wishing it were different, this is my good news—my wake-up truth!

It is good news in two ways: First, **he is in control.** Yay! I think God has done a pretty good job of running the universe so far, and there is no one else I would trust to take his place. Ever! Infinite love. Infinite wisdom. Infinite power.

The second reason it's good that "he changes the times and seasons" is that **I am not in control.** (And that is good news for everybody else too!) Not only do I not have to be in charge of everything, I cannot run the universe (much as I have tried).

So every time the seasons change, whether to drippy rain and falling leaves, or no rain and sweltering heat, we can take comfort that God is doing it. How reassuring that the planet is safely being guided continually by him in its dependable orbit around the sun.

And maybe he changes seasons just to remind us that he is God. And we are not.

I'm thankful the earth is still orbiting as designed, because the alternative certainly makes winter chill look appealing. And I will try to welcome the changing seasons in that light. Gratefully.

CHAPTER EIGHT

Spiritual Self-Care

Prayer:

Dear Lord, thank you that we can come to you any-time, anywhere, and in any shape. Help me draw near and open my heart as you nourish my weary soul.

Self-Care Is a Gift from God

When we're having a hard time, our natural instinct is to launch into self-preservation mode. Just do whatever it takes to survive!

Self-preservation is an instinct granted by God to much of his creation. But is there more? Are we destined to be consumed with the challenges of merely surviving, or can this fundamental self-preservation be enhanced and enriched?

The good news is that our Creator has gifted us with the privilege of making choices. *Beyond mere instinct lies the rich realm of self-care.* We're not talking about temporary luxuries, like manicures and super diets. True spiritual self-care—immersed in a personal relationship with the Lord—offers greater long-term value than simply surviving.

We have the option of thriving!

We can emerge on the other side of our deep valley with far more than we had when we entered it.

But we must make the choice.

Will we rely on our Creator and Great Shepherd to care for us? Will we choose to claim his amazing plans for us?

As you go through this day, stay aware of when you launch into human self-preservation, and choose that moment to reach out to the Lord. It's always by faith. He has set things up this way simply because he wants us close to himself.

> **For I know the thoughts that I think toward you, says the Lord, thoughts of peace and not of evil, to give you a future and a hope.** (Jeremiah 29:11)

Saturate Yourself with Scripture

Need a boost for your faith right now? God's Word is powerful. Supernatural!

The more our mind is on his promises and his truth, the more clearly things come into perspective and the easier it is to go on.

But to activate it, we have to soak it up. Not just gloss over it. Or as I tend to do: I think, *Oh, I know this one,* as I quickly skim over it. Then the verse stays only in my head and never makes it into my heart. ♥

Some people can spend hours reading scripture, and others, like me, can't sit still that long. Everyone is unique. The key is to get the Bible into our minds and hearts, then ruminate on it, not only all through the day, but also during those annoying wakeful moments at night, which you may surprisingly find are some of your most precious times with the Lord.

I encourage you to choose one verse or passage every morning to think about during the day. Write it down or put it somewhere where you'll see it often. Ask the Lord to speak to you through his Spirit, strengthen your faith, and bring you new blessings and insights that will transform you today. 🙂

Let the word of Christ dwell in you richly. (Colossians 3:16a)

Pour Out Your Heart to God in Prayer

Do you ever feel so overwhelmed when you come to God that you have no words? Or other times when you have so much to say that you hope he will hear you out?

There's no perfect way to approach God, except through his Son Jesus Christ. It was only by his sacrifice on the cross for us—and his eternal interceding on our behalf—that we are invited to come. ♥

Never before had anyone been able to access God, except through the high priest, and only with a blood sacrifice under the strictest conditions. We often take for granted that we can come to him anytime. Anywhere. In any condition.

Prayer is acknowledging and honoring God for who he is, asking for what we need; it is freedom to candidly express our emotions and continually cultivate closeness to our Savior.

No one can replace him in your heart. And no one can replace you in his.

As you pray throughout the day and night, pause before approaching his throne of grace with gratitude. And awe. Respond to his call to communicate in closeness with you. He is listening.

> **Let us therefore come boldly to the throne of grace, that we may obtain mercy and find grace to help in time of need.** (Hebrews 4:16)

Fill Your Mind with Wise and Positive Input

Clamor. Bad news. Negativity. Hopelessness. We're bombarded 24/7 with more input than any human was ever designed to process. How do we sort through it all? Or should we just unplug and be done?

Successful spiritual self-care requires ongoing nourishment from reliable sources. Who are the people in your life who are good for you? Who are the people who suck you dry and drag you down?

What are you seeing, reading, following, watching, and listening to? Stop and ask yourself: what leaves you feeling stronger, wiser, and more peaceful, and what leaves you anxious, angry, or stressed?

Remember we have the privilege—and responsibility—of choosing wisely.

Ask the Lord to show you today what to opt out of, unfollow, phase out of your life, or stop. And then ask him to lead you to the positive uplifting sources of truth and joy and wisdom that will truly ***nourish your soul.***

The change may be uncomfortable at first, and that is okay. But your choice will pay off!

Finally, brethren, whatever things *are* true, whatever things *are* noble, whatever things *are* just, whatever things *are* pure, whatever things *are* lovely, whatever things *are* of good report, if *there is* any virtue and if *there is* anything praiseworthy—meditate on these things. (Philippians 4:8)

Be Still . . . and Listen

Being still is so foreign to us! We're programmed to be in *go* mode. We believe that faster and busier is better!

Even as you read this, I wonder if you're thinking about what you'll do next. (I would be.) 😉

There's a good reason why God told us to be still. And along with it—to know that he is God. Worldly advice affirms that stillness is good, but sadly it leaves out the part about knowing he is God.

It feels normal to be on the move. Even when we do have down time, we overload our minds with nonstop stimulation. Most of us aren't even aware that we have enslaved ourselves to a state of perpetual fight or flight survival—adrenaline and all.

Our freedom comes from taking care of ourselves by choosing to be still and listen. But how?

Find a regular time every day. All alone. Get comfortable. Put on soothing music if it helps you relax or just revel in the bliss of silence. Breathe. Feel your body let go. Give yourself permission to not do anything.

Just be.

Then listen. Think about the Lord. Quote scripture if you want. Keep listening. It usually takes me about ten minutes to finally relax. To really be still.

Then listen for your Shepherd's voice. Because he loves you. ♥

My sheep hear My voice, and I know them, and they follow Me. (John 10:27)

Thank the Lord for the Blessings You Do Have

Funny how our minds tend to gravitate toward the negative, especially if it's something we feel compelled to fix. We might be experiencing a 97 percent blessing rate (humanly speaking), but all we can see is the other 3 percent.

Gratefulness is a choice. And although there are some people who actually seem to thrive on doom and gloom, I think most of us find freedom and joy in giving thanks.

However, it doesn't come naturally. Even David had to remind his soul to "bless the Lord," and not to forget all his benefits.

Gratefulness is the reward of choosing to give thanks—regardless of how challenging our circumstances.

What helps me is to focus on the three realms of blessings: **past, present, and future.** Whether you're on a walk, stuck in traffic, or chopping vegetables, anytime is a good time to count your blessings.

Start with something God has already done. **Thank him!**

Then take note of all the good things you see, taste, smell, hear, and feel right now. **Thank him!**

Finally, reflect on the promises he has given of future blessings. **Thank him!**

And the good news is that we will never ever run out of things for which to be grateful. 🙂

. . . giving thanks always for all things to God the Father in the name of our Lord Jesus Christ . . .
(Ephesians 5:20)

CHAPTER NINE

Tough Questions

Prayer:

Thank you, Lord, for revealing to us your truth in your Word. Please help us when we wrestle with tough questions to remember that our hope in you is sure and steadfast, because you are.

Why Do Some People Curse God, and Others Sing?

My blissful morning walk was suddenly disrupted when an angry man down the street was cursing God! Wow! Abruptly altering my route, I sadly wondered what had happened to cause such a vitriolic outburst.

A little later I saw a friend walking her dog, and she was smiling and singing. As she passed by, I commented, "So refreshing to hear singing!" She laughed and replied, "Oh, was I singing?" I assured her it was beautiful.

I happen to know that she was going through a very deep valley in her life. So I ask, **why is it that some people curse God, and others sing?**

Looking back through historical accounts in scripture, we see many occasions where people choose to reject God, refuse to give him honor and glory, and turn down his gift of love and mercy. And the more they do it, the harder their hearts become.

The ultimate tragedy is that eventually God gives them up (see Romans 1). What a frightening thought!

Intriguingly, we also see throughout time—and in many of our own lives—people who although they're suffering choose to respond in faith, believe God, honor Him, and receive His free gift of mercy and grace through Jesus Christ.

I doubt that most people begin their lives either cursing God or praising him. But most of us will end our lives doing one or the other. Of course, some people have harder lives than others, but no matter what we've endured, each of us makes choices along the way. And those choices will have one of only two possible destinations.

I love how God has graciously provided healing for our broken relationship with him, and how he never forces it down our throats. He is a God of grace, yet he also has given us freedom to choose or reject him.

I wonder if part of it is that he wants to have people with him forever who *want* to be with him.

And even then those of us who gladly choose to receive his free gift of eternal life through Jesus Christ know more than anyone how much we ourselves also need his grace and mercy. No boasting . . . ever!

Those who consistently reject the Lord, try harder and harder to find peace and joy and hope in the darkness of the absence of God. All in vain.

I don't know the odds of a person changing dramatically at the end of their life. But it seems that the more we consistently choose God and his way, the joy and peace and hope that come from having a **personal relationship with him brightens our lives like nothing else.**

And that is why we sing!

Does God Offer Soul Insurance?

Someone I know lost their home to a fire. Such a shock and tremendous loss! They were so grateful that at least they had a good fire insurance policy.

I got to wondering if God offers "soul insurance." I thought I knew the answer to that. But after some searching, you might be surprised at what I found.

None of us are strangers to the obligatory list of insurance policies: health, home, car, and even "life." Typically we talk with an agent first, and then sign up. There's no personal relationship with the rep—strictly a business transaction.

Then it's our responsibility to pay the premiums (ouch). And if we lapse in payments, so does our coverage. And that could prove to be a disaster.

Some religions offer "soul insurance." It might look something like this: You fulfill certain requirements, and in turn you have a better chance of going to Heaven (or other pleasant place) after death. Religions without relationship with God are very popular because they make people feel better.

God does *not* offer this counterfeit "soul insurance."

He offers something *far better!* I call it *Soul Assurance.* ☺

Here are three things he tells us in the scriptures:

1. It's based on a personal relationship with him. We know him and he knows us.

Jesus spoke of the coming judgment where people will plead with him and try to impress him with all the good things they did. His answer is, "I never knew you. Depart from Me." (Matthew 7:21-23) Truly tragic!

In contrast, I love that as our Good Shepherd, he said, "My sheep hear my voice, and I know them, … and I give to them eternal life." (John 10:27a,28a) ♥

2. Soul assurance is not dependent on what we do, but on the once-for-all price already paid by God's Son. It's a gift received by faith. With no premiums!

> For the wages of sin *is* death, but the gift of God *is* eternal life in Jesus Christ our Lord. (Romans 6:23)
>
> By grace you have been saved through faith; and this is not of yourselves, *it is* the gift of God; not a result of works, so that no one may boast. (Ephesians 2:8-9)

3. God's soul assurance is sure. Not wishful.

> "This *hope* we have as an anchor of the soul, both sure and steadfast, and which enters the *Presence* behind the veil . . . " (Hebrews 6:19)

The good news is that God doesn't offer soul "insurance," but **soul assurance.** An eternal policy paid in full! It's available to anyone through a personal relationship with him, by faith in the once-for-all payment of Jesus on the cross.

And that is the best policy anyone could ever have!

And this is eternal life, that they may know You, the only true God, and Jesus Christ whom You have sent. (John 17:3)

Eternal life is to *know him.* I hope you do.

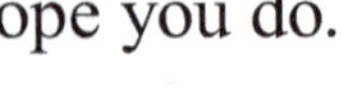

Can We Find God?

Golden retrievers have a way of making you feel like you are the most exciting, wonderful, perfect (and their favorite) person in the whole world! Lilly fit that bill. Adored by all her neighbors since the first day her owners tried to walk their new ball of fur, she won our hearts. She always made me laugh, so I called her Silly Lilly.

Until July 5. "Lilly is Missing!" posters were plastered everywhere. My heart sank. Freaked out by the fireworks, she panicked and ran. Prayers went up. I know her family was sick with grief. Everyone was searching for Lilly. With all their hearts!

When I came across this verse recently, it caught my attention:

"You will seek Me and find *Me* when you search for Me with all your heart." (Jeremiah 29:13)

I'd heard this many times but never paused to ponder what it might mean to me. The amazing truth is that God *wants* us to find him! He isn't hiding out hoping we can figure out how to find him or please him. The irony here is not that God is lost, but that *we are*. In fact, as Jesus, he became one of us, taking the punishment we deserve for our sins, and waits—longs—for us to turn to Him. He won't force anyone to believe.

So ask yourself three questions:

1. Do you *want* to find God?

It still surprises me, and saddens me, that many people do not want God. I can't even imagine what life now (or in eternity) would be like without him.

2. Where are you looking?

This world offers a lot of counterfeit god-like attractions, many of which might be good but still fall vastly short of God himself. Only in his Word (the Bible) can we find his truth. The more we read and hear his Word, the more our faith grows. And day and night his mighty power and deity are displayed for all to see in his amazing creation.

3. How will you know if/when you've found him?

Because finding and knowing God is a supernatural phenomenon, there are no simple formulas, religious rituals, or "three easy steps." The key is our heart. An intimate relationship with the God of the universe requires trusting him with all our heart.

Because he promises to indwell believers with his Holy Spirit, you may find yourself more loving, peaceful, and joyful (see Galatians 5:22). And because it is a relationship, you may find yourself talking with him about everything, and also learning to listen. You might start to sing more. And notice his love messages to you through his written Word, his creation, or people.

Because God is infinite, we will have eternity to get to know him more and more. He has put a hunger and thirst in us to increasingly delight in him! As the song goes, "We've only just begun."

Guess who I saw walking down the street on July 7th? Lilly was found! Their heartfelt search was successful! And Lilly had the biggest smile I've ever seen! 🙂

"You will seek Me and find Me when you search for Me with all your heart." (Jeremiah 29:13) ♥

Birth Pangs and Death: Curse or Hope?

Today we lost a dear brother. No matter how prepared we may be, death always takes us off guard. And rightly so. What puzzles me, however, was that although he was ready to go (he told us just a few days ago that he had perfect peace, and was trusting Jesus to take him Home soon), yet he still had to writhe in pain and agony at the very end. *Why?*

Why do some people slip off quietly, yet so many others suffer?

If Jesus died for our sin and promises to carry us safely Home to be with him, can't he also make that transition itself pleasant and painless?

Today we also got news of a new baby born to another dear family. So much joy! Despite the pain and agony of childbirth.

Then it hit me! It all ties together and makes sense! God is working his perfect plan. After Adam and Eve rebelled against God, among the very first things God said to them was that women will have pain in childbirth. I always assumed this was just a random punishment (along with weeds and work). Not at all!

God does nothing randomly. This was a picture for us, part of his plan to redeem us and make a way for us to come back home to him. He also promised them that a Savior would come.

We have hope!

Written centuries later, Paul in Romans 8:22–23 explains, "For we know that the whole creation groans and labors with birth pangs together until now. Not only *that*, but we also who have the firstfruits of the Spirit, even we ourselves groan within ourselves, eagerly waiting for the adoption, the redemption of our body."

It has been part of God's plan all along to give us an ongoing reminder of not only the *seriousness of our sin* (pain and death—paralleling childbirth) but also the *hope that he offers* (eternal life after death—paralleling the new life in the newborn child.) ♥

So the groaning we all experience is just a necessary doorway as we leave these death-doomed bodies to go on either to life with him in Heaven, or eternal torment without him in hell. Jesus offered no other options.

The good news is that birth pangs are temporary, both for the mother as well as the baby, and lead to life and unimaginable joy!

So every time you hear of a newborn child, or a loved one who has died, remember that *God does have it covered.* He wants us to not get too comfortable in this fallen world and these failing bodies of ours. But to rest our hope fully on his promises and the finished saving work of Jesus Christ on the cross—*for us*!

Going to go pull some weeds now, and then go greet a new baby. 🙂

How Can You Say That God Is Good?

It's so easy to say "God is good!" when things are going well. And I deeply admire those who also say it when things are *not* going well. But does that even make sense? Can God be good and yet allow bad things?

We all struggle with questions like these, especially those of us who've seen and been through horrific things.

Over the centuries, volumes have been written addressing this apparent disparity, but I just want to share what helps me make sense of it. One word: perspective. *Am I focusing on this fleeting moment, or am I forward-focused on what will last forever?* Which really has the supreme value?

What if God did give us everything we wanted right now in this life, but no promises for after we die. At first that sounds like winning the lottery! But when you connect the dots, eventually at some point in time, it will all end. *Then what?*

Wouldn't you rather have a good God who has the love and the power to give us everything we could ever want *forever*, after we die, but who allows us to go through hard times now for some reason he's not obligated to explain?

To me, his goodness lies not in any temporary favors (although those are truly blessings too!), but in the fact that he has done everything to give us all we'll ever need and want in his kingdom.

God's goodness is showcased by the fact that Jesus willingly suffered and died so the gift of eternal life would be free to all who receive him by faith. This ultimate victorious display of goodness over evil's darkness should greatly overshadow any doubts.

In the meantime, everyone who gets to Heaven by God's grace will have been through hard times. In this life we all have challenges to overcome. But rest assured that when we are on the other side, with him, it *will be worth it all.*

And there we will have plenty of time to talk about how good God is!

***I would have lost heart,* unless I had believed**
That I would see the goodness of the LORD
In the land of the living.
(Psalm 27:13)

Halloween: Who and What Are We Celebrating?

I got a shock today that disrupted my typically calm and rejuvenating morning walk. Praising God and enjoying the breathtaking autumn splendor, suddenly I saw a skull and hand bones piercing up out of the ground! Witches, tombstones, ghosts, dead body parts, spiders, and snakes…all decorating someone's front lawn! Triggered and repulsed, I ran as fast as I could.

Later I ran into a friend walking her dog. She remarked that her sweet calm dog got very upset and frightened by the yard decorations. How intriguing that animals sense and tremble at what humans make light of!

Topping it all off, a little neighbor girl showed me the book her parents just gave her—all about zombies.

Why do people think death and evil are fun, or humorous, or worth celebrating? Do they not believe it is real, or do they just truly love it?

Personally, I enjoy dressing up and having fun. One of my most memorable Halloween costumes was in college when I dressed up as a sassy space alien, complete with green food coloring on my face. Smashing success and great fun—until I went to wash my face that night. Oops! Had to go back to school the next day with a lot of explaining to do. (Fun fact: food coloring is as effective as using a Sharpie.) 😆

Unfortunately, this popular holiday is an opportunity for many to feature the occult, death, evil, blood, skeletons, graveyards, and numerous other ghoulish horrors. These themes are the exact opposite of all that we as Christ-followers celebrate every spring at Easter!

The contrast is stark: evil vs. good, death vs. life, darkness vs. light, deception vs. truth, sadness vs. joy, despair vs. hope, fear vs. peace, Satan vs. Jesus.

In the absence of a *solid source of truth*, people have no reason to not celebrate something else. In the absence of a *personal relationship* with our Creator and Savior, people have no reason not to celebrate an impostor. Whatever feels good at the time too often wins out.

Without the truth and without the Savior, the tragedy is that it ends up unimaginably worse than any gruesome lawn decor could ever portray.

Ultimately each of us has to choose who and what we celebrate.

And that choice will carry us to one of only two eternal destinations: Heaven or Hell.

The good news is that according to God's truth (the Bible) we have hope! There's hope for something beyond the grave for all who choose to believe and receive His free gift of forgiveness and eternal life.

Now that is worth celebrating!

Here are a few promises from Jesus himself:

For God so loved the world that He gave His only begotten Son, that whoever believes in Him should not perish but have everlasting life. (John 3:16)

He who believes in the Son has everlasting life; and he who does not believe the Son shall not see life, but the wrath of God abides on him. (John 3:36)

Jesus said to her, "I am the resurrection and the life. He who believes in Me, though he may die, he shall live. And whoever lives and believes in Me shall never die. Do you believe this?" (John 11:25–26)

Jesus said to him, "I am the way, the truth, and the life. No one comes to the Father except through Me." (John 14:6)

"In My Father's house are many mansions; if *it were* not *so*, I would have told you. I go to prepare a place for you. And if I go and prepare a place for you, I will come again and receive you to Myself; that where I am, *there* you may be also." (John 14:2-3)

I hope we can all be more mindful all year round of who and what we choose to celebrate. Why? Because I can't imagine any other option as amazing as what our Lord offers! ♥

CHAPTER TEN

Learning Curves

Prayer:

Dear Lord, thank you that you love us and know what's best for us, even if it doesn't always feel wonderful at the time. Please help us embrace your goodness as we learn and grow on this journey.

Boy, Did I Blow It!

Have you ever made such a colossal mistake that you thought, "*This* is one booboo even God can't fix!"? I recently erroneously emailed the wrong document to a very important person. Oops! Huge mistake and repercussions! When it hit me, I freaked out, prayed for a "take it back!" button, tried not to say bad words, and almost threw up.

Whether a deliberate choice that backfires or an unintentional error, we *all* make mistakes. We beat ourselves up for being human, and we panic about the messes we've made.

Can God fix them, and does he?

I take great comfort in the promise that says, "And we know that all things work together for good to those who love God, to those who are the called according to *His* purpose" (Romans 8:28).

It's taken me years to notice what Romans 8:28 does *not* say:

And we know that God (not me) **causes** (not by chance) **all things** (not just some things) **to work together for good** (not necessarily for us to always feel good about it) **to those who love God, to those who are called** (not for everyone but for followers of Jesus) **according to His purpose** (not so we can have everything the way we want right now, but ultimately for the big picture.)

And more good news is that not only can we apply this supernatural treasure to our own mistakes, but we can also use it in our lives when other people do something wrong toward us. (Hmmm. That's a little harder.)

In fact, it's a bit ironic that the massively blatant "mistake" of crucifying the Son of God turned out to be our ultimate blessing, all aligned with God's eternal purpose, resulting in good for us and glory for him.

Although we may never see the "good" that God has worked in every situation, we can rest assured that **He loves us,** and that **He knows** what is best for us, and that **He is capable** of carrying that out in his time and his way.

So let's relax more, do our best, and let him make the most of it…mistakes and all.

Judger or Pray-er?

Ever find yourself wondering why someone acts like they do, or looks like they do? *If only they would ____________!*

I recently caught myself on autopilot in judging mode. Well, there were a bunch of people I could have helped. Or so I assumed. Isn't that my job?

But this time was different. Like an uncomfortable wake-up call, long overdue, I realized I didn't *want* to be a judger!

In addition to the fact that the Lord warns us not to judge, I really don't like how it feels.

So how do I break free from the bondage of habitually judging others? Here's what's helping me:

1. Confess my pride

God is the only one who is qualified to judge. And that's because he's perfect, and all-knowing. I am neither. Not even close!

And it also humbles me to realize that others might be judging me too. *Why does she do that? And why does she look like that?* 😆

2. Change criticism to compassion

Have I ever paused to ponder what that person might be going through, or might have been through?

Or what they're feeling deep down?

3. Choose to pray

If I want to be a pray-er rather than a judger, this is what I *can* do. Every time I catch myself slipping into critical mode, I can pause to pray for them, right then and there:

Lord, I pray for that person.
I don't know what they've been through.

I don't know what they're going through.
I don't know what they need.
But I know we all need you.
Please help them come to know you as their Savior and Lord.
And please be to them everything they need.
Amen.

Lotta people gonna get prayed for!
I like how that feels. 🙂

" ... man looks at the outward appearance, but the LORD looks at the heart." (1 Samuel 16:7) ♥

The Cry of My Heart

Recently I messaged a dear friend who, for as long as I've known her, has struggled with health and mobility, and I never heard one word of complaint. (She would have heard a few words from me if the roles were reversed! 😉) After asking her how she was, she replied:

"I love the old songs: 'Show me Your ways, that I may walk with You. Show me Your ways, I put my hope in You. The cry of my heart is to love You more, to live with the touch of Your hand. Stronger each day, show me Your ways.' I just love this song!" *

Yesterday a massive stroke suddenly took her life. The cry of her heart at last is totally and eternally fulfilled. Donna now has forever to love and walk with the Lord, and to feel his loving touch.

In the wake of death's sting, I paused to reflect:

What is the cry of *my* heart?

Most of my life it has been: "Lord fix this!" "Heal this!" "Give me this!" Can I honestly say my very deepest longing is just to know him? Love him? Walk with him?

There's nothing wrong with asking for what we want. Jesus spoke often of coming to the Father for what we need, and we are encouraged all through scripture to pray. But if that is as far as we go, are we missing the real treasure?

Imagine for a minute that God does answer all your prayers and gives you everything you request. A hundred years from now, will it matter?

And now imagine if all you asked for was to know him and love him and walk with him? If he himself was the deepest cry of your heart?

A hundred years from now, that will have more value than anything else we could ever ask or think!

And the blessings start here and now.

This is where I'd like to give you a list of three things to do to have Jesus be the deepest cry of your heart. But I can't. It's not about a to-do list. All I can say is I'm pretty sure it starts with choosing him . . . over and over. And responding to his love messages to us. Every moment of every day.

I encourage you to listen to the song. I know now why Donna loved it so much: *because* she loved her *Savior!* ♥
*("Show Me Your Ways" by Darlene Zschech—Hillsong, 1996)

Three Tips for Reclaiming Joy & Peace in Turbulent Times

(Written during the Pandemic of 2020)

On the verge of physical and emotional collapse, I recently arrived back home after my final emergency trip to be with my dear dying mother. Rejoicing that she was safely Home with the Lord, yet exhausted on every level, I was grateful that now I had time to rest, heal, and replenish—with no stress. That very day all the stuff hit the fan!

Why is it that just when we think we can't take any more, the Lord often has other plans?

I've been struggling along with everyone else with all the turbulence, compounded by personal grief and loss. I've hit bottom more than once, yet I am finally starting to rise above it all.

Here are a few things that have been helping me, not to merely survive, but actually begin to *reclaim God's joy and peace.*

1. Release expectations and entitlements.

We need to unclench our fists, open our hands, and let go of what we thought it would or should be. The prophet Habakkuk was preparing to lose everything in an imminent enemy invasion. After much wrestling, he was finally able to let go, releasing his demand for earthly comforts, and choosing to cling to God and his eternal promise of salvation. No matter what may happen.

Though the fig tree may not blossom,
Nor fruit be on the vines;
Though the labor of the olive may fail,
And the fields yield no food;
Though the flock may be cut off from the fold,
And there be no herd in the stalls—
Yet I will rejoice in the Lord,
I will joy in the God of my salvation.
(Habakkuk 3:17–18)

2. Open your senses to all the good that is around you now.

When was the last time you stepped outside and just listened to the birds sing? Or actually stopped to smell a fragrant flower? Or gazed at the moon or stars?

This morning I listened to Christmas music, and found myself dancing in the kitchen! 🙂

With so much nonstop toxicity bombarding us, we need to choose to refocus on all the goodness the Lord is showering upon us. To physically take in and savor our blessings. Now. In spite of what we may not have at the moment.

Oh, taste and see that the Lord *is* good;
Blessed *is* the man *who* trusts in Him!
(Psalm 34:8)

3. Actively seek God and his truth.

Between news, social media, and our own unreliable minds, it's easy to feel depressed, confused, fearful, and angry. We desperately want answers to our questions and solutions to the problems. But the harder we try, the deeper down we seem to spiral.

Even people of faith are struggling. And possibly feeling guilty about not being instantly victorious in the battle.

Heartbroken and deeply grieving as I watched my mom shrivel up, one of the most encouraging things was to cling to God's Word. And having written *Goodbye for Now*, a book to support those losing a loved one, I was able to read to her the scripture verses in it about salvation and Heaven.

Just hearing the promises strengthened my faith—and hers—in a very fearful and unfamiliar time.

The Lord never promised that we would understand what he is doing, or why. But when we choose to seek him, and stop to listen to what he says, our faith is strengthened, and his peace supernaturally overrides our fears. ♥

"But seek first the kingdom of God and His righteousness, and all these things shall be added to you." (Matthew 6:33)

Many of us pray the Lord's Prayer, specifically, "Thy will be done." It never occurred to me that perhaps *his will is being done!* The supreme example in history was Jesus's death on the cross for us. In that moment, it looked like God was gone, unloving, or out of control.

But now we see that it was his plan all along. And those who receive him will one day be with him forever in **endless joy and peace.** (And there we will never run out of food, money, or bath tissue!)

In Search of the Perfect Place to Live

It seems like the older we get, the more we dream about and search for the ideal place to live. Beach-paradise Hawaii . . . tropical, lazy Florida . . . sunny, exciting California . . . rural, relaxing Montana . . . the Greek islands . . . mountain-peaked Colorado . . . beautiful British Columbia . . . and on it goes.

But not for long. We soon discover that every place has its hurricanes, snowstorms, droughts, earthquakes, crime . . . and on it goes.

Some people are fortunate to reap the benefits of multiple locations, such as arid Arizona in the winter and the cool Northwest in the summer. But even then, there is no place that I know of that is perfect . . . here on earth anyway.

Looking back in time, we can see that originally there was a perfect place to live. Adam and Eve had it all. But unfortunately, they didn't think so. And tragically they rebelled against the loving God who had given them everything a human being could ever want or need.

As a result, the human race and the earth we inhabit are under a curse until the promised time of a new Heaven and new Earth.

Although there's no perfect place to live here now, the good news is that it's coming for all who believe in Jesus and his substitutionary death on the cross for us.

He promised that he was going to prepare a place for us. And according to the scriptures, the new layout will *far surpass* the original one, which we know was amazing!

I still enjoy dreaming about a better place to live here, and keep my ears and eyes open for any well-kept-secret towns.

But I'm not on hold waiting for one, and realize that even if I did find "it," it would only be temporary at best.

So for today I'm going to count the blessings I *do* have here in this imperfect world, and enjoy thinking about what that future perfect place might be like. At least no matter where I am, I *know who is with me.*

And he is what makes any place perfect.

"I go to prepare a place for you . . . that where I am, *there* you may be also." ~Jesus (John 14:2b,3b)

Tapping into Supernatural Realms

Stupid, annoying traffic jam! The freeway was at a standstill, so my husband and I cleverly decided to take the side road. Oops. Bad idea. (Everyone else was clever too).

So we detoured over to another route but found it to be even worse! The radio update chalked it all up to an accident. Bummer. After grumbling all the way—and hitting all the red lights—I was so glad to finally be home. What a day!

Three hours later, it occurred to me that someone had been in a terrible accident! Wow. I was so consumed with my own discomfort that compassion never occurred to me. So I stopped right then and prayed for the people involved, whoever they were.

We're told to pray for others, but do we? In my opinion, praying is not always fun. It takes effort. And time.

Revisiting the account of Jesus in the garden just hours before his tortuous murder on our behalf, in indescribable agony, do you know what he was doing? *Praying for us!* And I'm pretty sure it was not fun. But I am so glad he did!

We too should pray for others more, just as if they were our own loved ones.

When God brings a person to mind, we can pause for a moment and lift them up. When we hear a siren, we can offer a prayer for the people involved. When someone posts a need on social media, we can stop and actually talk to the Lord about it.

It may not be fun, and it will take a minute. But it should blow us away to realize we have the *awesome privilege of coming before the God of the universe* because of the sacrifice of his Son Jesus, who opened up the way for us!

I hope someone else is there to pray for me when I need it.

And isn't it amazing to know we can tap into supernatural realms at any moment to do something that really will make a difference!

"Let us therefore come boldly to the throne of grace, that we may obtain mercy and find grace to help in time of need." (Hebrews 4:16) ♥

CHAPTER ELEVEN

Heart Warmers

Prayer:

Thank you, Lord, for blessing us with your amazing love and joy. Please flow through us to warm the hearts of those around us and bring you joy.

Puppy Love

I'd always had and loved dogs, and they love me. Shared playful moments, cuddles, beds, and even a few fleas. I delight in the memories, including our adorable Basset who flunked obedience training, the regal Great Dane who cowered when the kitten raised its paw, and the faithful Golden Retriever who brought home a pair of giant boxer shorts belonging to the neighbor (we didn't return them). 😆

Now in this season of life, I'm dogless by choice. As much as I miss having a dog of my own, I am still enjoying them every day!

Over the years, my morning neighborhood walks have transformed me into a sort of dog whisperer. Cats, on the other hand, are more of a hit-or-miss challenge. But dogs? When they see me coming, they start wigglin' and waggin'!

Recently, I started carrying dog treats, which have received rave rover reviews. And 100 percent repeat business! I even got one dog to sit, much to the surprise of his owner. "He can sit???" And to be polite, I always offer a treat to the owners too—but no takers yet.

I also cherish the human interaction—lots of laughs, new acquaintances and budding friendships. And perhaps even more touching are the moments shared with those who feel safe enough to bare their hearts. So many people, and those they love, are hurting.

How precious is the privilege of connecting and caring.

Sometimes, I even wrap them in a hug, and a promise to hold them in my heart and prayers. 💜

The other beautiful blessing born from all this is an ongoing neighborhood support and encouragement group. And of course, most of them have dogs!

What I've been discovering is two-fold:

1) When we feel something missing in our lives, open our hearts to the blessings we do have.

2) And when we give love and joy, not only does it spread to and through others, but it always comes back around to warm our own hearts more than we ever imagined.

" ... the love of God has been poured out in our hearts by the Holy Spirit who was given to us." (Romans 5:5b) ♥

Wanna Buy a Painted Rock?

Ya gotta love enterprising kids who have lemonade stands, peddle their worn-out toys, and endeavor to get rich by selling you a rock from their backyard. That was Marcus.

Hoping for an easy sale as I walked by his house, he called out exuberantly, "Wanna buy a rock?"

Not one to be rushed into high pressure sales, I countered, "How much?"

"Two bucks." He sounded pretty firm.

Glancing at my pockets I sadly replied, "I don't have two bucks."

He had no intention of letting this sale slip by. "How much *do* you have?"

Checking my pockets to see what kind of bartering power I might have, I had one final offer.

"I have a dog biscuit."

Pausing—probably just to make me sweat, he then lit up with a smile from cheek to cheek, "Okay!"

Then grabbing a little rock, he asked me what I wanted him to paint on it. Although thoroughly amused by this time, I was eager to resume my walk. So I thought of the quickest picture he could draw.

"How 'bout a happy face?"

Ten seconds later, the masterpiece was complete. I held the rock in my hand and raved, "This is beautiful, Marcus. I love it! It makes me happy."

He beamed.

"And you know what else makes me happy?"

"What?"

"Jesus." 🙂

Totally puzzled, his face went blank.

"He's the one who made this rock, and made you, and your dog, and the stars, and everything! And he loves you."

"Oh."

So I thanked him again and was on my way.

~~~~~~~~~~~~~~~~~~~~~~~~

Sitting here now, enjoying the happy rock, I still chuckle at the young boy's exuberance. In addition to the sheer joy of the whole interaction, I'm grateful for the opportunity to encourage and affirm this budding artistic entrepreneur.

And most of all, to be able to plant a small seed in his heart. I pray he goes on in his life to seek a relationship with his Creator and Savior. ♥

I'm also enjoying the fact that I'm richer than I realized—I have a whole bag of dog biscuits!

~~~~~~~~~~~~~~~~~~~~~~~~

School Is Almost Out!

One of my all-time favorite memories is of the last week of school, from kindergarten to college graduation, and even more so as a teacher. 😉 Nothing better than having work done, and summer vacation almost here!

Walking past a school today, I felt that exuberance of anticipation!

As I wished that we could have that feeling forever, it dawned on me that perhaps we can.

Although no one knows the exact date they will die, as believers we can and should live as if we are in the final season—like the last week of school. Because of God's proven love for us in sending Jesus to suffer and die in our place, and then rise again, the eternal summer vacation has been scheduled for us by his grace.

In pondering this, several things come to mind:

1. Looking back: It's easy to forget how far we've come, all we've learned, the challenges we've overcome, the mistakes we've made, and God's faithfulness all along. Pausing to reflect can be a real encouragement, especially if we are in the middle of a discouraging time.

2. Cleaning out: How fun to throw things away that we once thought were so important! The farther along we get in life, the more we realize what truly has value, and what does not.

3. Cherishing relationships: Remember signing yearbooks? All the silly and mushy things we wrote for our friends! In our later seasons of life, we come to cherish those who are precious to us and pray we too will be cherished by others.

4. Finishing up: As in school where there are often last-minute tasks to be completed, so in life we have before us things we want to accomplish before we go. I pray the Lord will show me what those things are, and that he will help me complete them successfully. And that I will stay open to the work he wants to complete *in me* as well.

5. Looking forward: Although as finite humans limited to four space-time dimensions, we can barely grasp the promises God has given us, he has revealed more than enough to make us feel secure, excited, and hopeful for what he has in store for us.

The words of Jesus in the books of John and Revelation remind us that our ultimate graduation—and heavenly summer vacation—is just around the corner.

And we don't have to go back to school in the fall! 🙂

I Love You Too!

Do you remember the first time someone special said, "I love you" and you could hardly wait to respond with a heartfelt "I love you too!" Not much in this life compares to the rapture of that moment.

And when you think about it, not much compares to the risk—the torturous anxiety—of that eternity between the "I love you" and the response. What if they laugh? Or slap me? Or ignore me as if they had not heard? Or perhaps the worst, the dreaded "I like you, but let's just be friends." Ouch!

The good news is that with God, he has already taken the risk. When Jesus willingly submitted to his own torturous death on the cross, *in our place,* **he was looking at you and saying, "I love you."** It's our privilege to respond!

But how do you say, "I love you too" to God? It can feel very awkward. Almost trite. But when we express our devotion to him in the context of response to his display of affection on the cross, it seems so right.

Love full circle. Like he meant it to be all along!

I'm finally realizing that although with God sometimes we do have rapturous moments, we don't need to experience them continually in our relationship with him. The simplicity of his love and our response is all we need. "We love Him because He first loved us" (I John 4:19).

He said it first. We have the privilege of responding.

When was the last time you told God that you loved him too? Perhaps we all can *not only tell him, but even better, show him.*

And that brings rapture to his heart.

"In this is love, not that we loved God, but that He loved us and sent His Son to *be* the propitiation for our sins." (I John 4:10) ♥

Spring Is Coming!

Fall used to scare me. Not the creepy costumes, sticky spider webs, or glucose overdoses. What can cause a chill of fright in me is that the days ahead will be short, dark, and cold. And sometimes lonely.

Several years ago, I looked outside at the drippy cold November day. I felt damp inside. Overwhelmed. As the rain poured off the flowerless shrubs, I wasn't sure if I could endure one more depressing winter.

Suddenly in my mind flashed a bright burst of springy scarlet blooms!

It was as if the Lord was saying, *"Don't be afraid. Spring is coming!"* And it did.

That vivid scarlet vision, wrapped in his timeless promises, carried me through.

I've learned that when I sit with the Lord in the dark, in my pain, *he is there.* Just as he promised. Along with his peace and comfort.

Now each year as winter draws near, I refresh my memory with that hope-filled spring image. It helps not only for the impending physical and emotional winters ahead in this life, but also for the moments I feel wobbly about my eternal future.

Each of us chooses who or what we hang our soul on. The only solid actual historical event worthy of my trust is the death and resurrection of Jesus Christ. That was a real physical manifestation of God's boundless love for us.

His love was written in red.

And just as I believe that he died and rose again for me, so I hang all the weight of my soul and my future on that fact.

As the bright scarlet blooms give me hope for a coming spring, so the blood of Jesus gives me hope for an inconceivably amazing future with my Lord!

And even if the flowers do not bloom, or if __________ (fill in the blank) . . . , I will rejoice in the God of my salvation! (Habakkuk 3:17–19, paraphrase)

He is my hope! ♥

100,000 Answered Prayers!

"100,000 answered prayers!" was the answer. What was the question?

Here's what happened:

Several years ago, I was facing a horrendous challenge in my life. (Aren't they all?) 😉 Even after praying fervently many times, I still had this nagging doubt. "Of course the Lord has answered many of my prayers in the past, but this is different. This just may be the one that he can't or won't fix."

In my wobbling and wrestling, somewhere along the way I decided to try to calculate how many prayers the Lord had answered so far in my life. Technically, he answers every prayer with a "Yes," a "No" or a "Maybe." But I was just interested in the "Yes" answers.

For starters, there were all the times I prayed first thing in the morning, before leaving the house, before making a phone call or sending an email. I've prayed daily for many people. I prayed before every test, every solo, and every piano performance. I prayed many prayers about the young men in my life (or lack thereof). Health issues, money matters, disappointments, loved ones, huge decisions—and much more—have brought me to my knees.

Pretty amazed at that point, I decided to do the math: all those prayers multiplied by how many days I've been walking this earth.

And I came up with about 100,000!

I wrote it down on a yellow sticky note and put it on the refrigerator.

100,000 Answered Prayers!

Looking at that note continues to lift my spirit and warm my heart. It encourages me to keep on asking. And thanking him.

Fast-forward to last week, at a neighborhood women's group, a discussion question was asked: What saying do you have on your wall that encourages you?

100,000 Answered Prayers!

Prayer is simply meeting with God, cherishing and growing in our relationship with him.

And I see now that many of the prayers that were a "No," turned out for the best in the long run.

God is good. And he is faithful.

Sometimes looking back helps us look forward.

"The prayer of the upright *is* His delight."
(Proverbs 15:8b)

CHAPTER TWELVE

Stress Busters

Prayer:

Dear Jesus, Prince of Peace, thank you for your comfort, calming and quieting love. Please help us let go, be still, and know that you are our God. Forever.

Word to the Worrywart

Remember waaaay back to your first date? I was so excited when Dan T. asked me to the senior banquet! And then I panicked. *Oh no! The front seat of his car is a bench seat. Where do I sit?*

The happy butterflies quickly morphed into the urge to barf.

With not enough time to consult Ann Landers, I immediately sought counsel from my wise friends. *If I sit right next to him,* we reasoned, *it might be too forward. But if I sit next to the door, I might seem aloof.* My anxiety hit the roof as we continued to deliberate.

That evening I felt a gentle nudge. "*Welby, have you prayed about it?*"

Wow. God is even concerned about things like this. So I did. Funny, but I felt a little better.

The next day a unanimous verdict finally came in from the friends: I would sit right where the glove box ended. Sort of in the middle. So relieved! We finally had it all figured out.

Or so I thought.

As the day grew nearer, I still wrestled with worry. All the what ifs! Funny how our brains can generate such a menagerie of wild scenarios!

If only I had something I could *do* instead of worry.

Well, date night finally came, and I was as ready as I could be. So grateful that at least I knew the Lord was with me.

Heart pounding and deodorant failing, I saw his car approach. He was halfway up the driveway when I realized it was a different car! Greeting me he explained that he borrowed the car from a friend. He opened the door for me, and as I climbed in, I burst out laughing!

This car had bucket seats! 😆

Well, now that I've had about a hundred years to laugh, and reflect, I've learned a few things. Whether a first date or something life threatening—or anything in between—we all wrestle with worry.

We know it's not helpful, and most of us are familiar with all the clever sayings. But other than attempting to just reason it away, is there actually *something I can do to* help triumph over the anxiety?

The Apostle Paul answered that question as he wrote this from prison, suffering for his faith in Jesus. In the middle of his life-threatening fear he wrote: "*Be anxious for nothing, but...*" (Philippians 4:6a).

"but" – but WHAT???

Here it is:

"... but in everything by prayer and supplication, with thanksgiving, let your requests be made known to God." (Philippians 4:6)

In the moment, when we're overwhelmed and can't see any hope, we can *pray and give thanks* to our loving, wise, gracious, all-powerful God!

I also love these Worrywart antidotes:

"*. . . casting all your care upon Him, for He cares for you.*" (1 Peter 5:7)

"*You will keep* him *in perfect peace,*
Whose *mind* is *stayed on* You,
Because he trusts in You." (Isaiah 26:3)

Here are three things I've learned:

1. It's not just "saying a prayer" or "giving thanks," but it's the relationship—connecting with God—that's the true treasure. 

2. Remember that praying to the Lord and thanking him are not a substitute for healthcare interventions. However, our relationship with him is the foundational core of everything else we need.

3. And the best news, the triumphant promise:

"[After you pray and give thanks] . . . **the peace of God, which surpasses all understanding, will guard your hearts and minds through Christ Jesus."** (Philippians 4:7)

Yay! That's one less wart to worry about. 

Take a Rubber Band Vacation

Do you fall into bed exhausted, but your brain won't shut off? Feel like life keeps getting busier and faster? Wonder just how much more you can s-t-r-e-t-c-h?

I love rubber bands. Last week I lost one of my favorites due to overstretching. I guess it had been too tight for too long. And it snapped!

Gazing at a pile of new relaxed rubber bands, it hit me. If rubber bands need a little rest, or vacation, to avoid snapping, how much more do we!

Several years ago I bottomed out, battling for my life for over a year. All due to a perfect storm of multiple factors, one of which was me pushing too hard for too long. Just power through! Worked for a while. Then I snapped.

I always assumed if I slowed down, I'd lose my momentum, and just be too tired to accomplish anything. And the supreme goal is to do as much as you can and do it well, right? My adrenaline-charged overactive brain was a harsh taskmaster; but I didn't know any differently.

It took a total collapse (doctors didn't think I'd make it) until I was able to slowly start turning the ship around. And that was only possible by the grace of God, to whom I am forever grateful.

A key part of my recovery has been learning to take mini "vacations" throughout the day, and retraining my brain and body to cherish the stillness. Ahhh. I never knew how good it could feel to relax. Recharge. Reflect. Rest.

I've gained a new appreciation for the Lord's words: "Be still, and know that I *am* God." (Psalm 46:10)

This about-face totally saved—and changed—my life! I'm happier, calmer, and sleeping better than ever!

Here are three takeaways that have made a significant difference:

1. Take Heed of Warning Signs

Warning signs could be any number of things: headache, indigestion, difficulty sleeping, irritability, feeling driven or overwhelmed, a sense of urgency or hurry, shallow breathing, etc. And often I don't realize how wound up I am until I stop, sit down, breathe, and be still.

2. Take a Mini Vacation Every Day

This might be tough for some, but it's essential to find a safe quiet place all alone. Get comfy. I love my cozy recliner, but even a parked car will do. This is a conscious retraining of the brain and body to slow down, and operate in rest and digest mode, rather than fight or flight.

Let yourself *just be* in one of your favorite places (real or imagined): maybe basking in the sun on a tropical beach, or lounging by a peaceful pool, or stargazing on a summer night. *Just be.* Take pleasure in the fresh air and warm sun, soft sand and gentle waves, cheery birds or calming crickets. Breathe slowly and deeply. Dream of Heaven. Let thankfulness flow freely. Rest in the comforting arms of your Good Shepherd, Heavenly Father, and Prince of Peace.

When your mind starts bombarding you with all the things you need to do right now, just smile, and go back to that beautiful place.

You might start to notice some belly gurgles, which is a sign that your brain has successfully transitioned to rest and digest (parasympathetic). Yay! That is a victory! And when you do decide to get back to your tasks, you'll probably feel more energized but in a calm way. Just like a relaxed rubber band. 🙂

I do this twice a day, for 15–30 minutes, usually morning and evening. The evening quietness is such a peaceful preparation for bedtime.

3. Take an All-Day Vacation Every Week

It's a big commitment you'll never regret! A friend of mine calls it her "protected day." Some call it a Sabbath. You choose what day of the week you will regularly set aside for self-care.

What do you need to do, and not do, *for you*? What will help you be totally relaxed and peaceful and happy all day?

For me it's turning off the laptop. No emails, no texts. No appointments or obligations. The calendar is clear. And I just make it up as I go along! Sleep, eat, go for walks, watch a movie, read a book, file my nails, look out the window, call a friend if I want, etc. And I also include my regular mini vacations as well.

It's amazing how refreshed I feel. And I look forward to the next vacation!

Don't wait until you snap. Every time you see a rubber band, ask yourself if you need a little vacation. Let go often, trust God, and rest in your Prince of Peace.♥

Self-care is not a luxury. It's a lifeline. Just ask a rubber band.

Those who wait on the Lord
Shall renew their strength;
They shall mount up with wings like eagles,
They shall run and not be weary,
They shall walk and not faint. (Isaiah 40:31)

Want Peace?

I love Amazon! And I also adore the lady who delivers to us! One day I asked her if she had any prayer requests. After giving it some thought, she replied, "Peace."

What a great request! Pretty sure we all want peace. But how many of us have it, and know how to find it?

Do you want someone to calm you when everything feels like it's spinning out of control?

Do you want someone to comfort you when you're writhing in pain and grief?

Do you want someone to soothe you when you wake anxiously in the night?

Do you want someone to reassure you that everything is going to be all right?

Do you want someone to give you rest in your weariness?

Because we were created for a personal relationship with the glorious God of the universe, it's innate to long for peace. But as a result of our own sin, tragically that relationship is severed—separating us from the only one who can give us deep lasting peace.

This broken world can't even come close to satisfying our hearts with genuine permanent peace. Neither can we find its source inside ourselves, though we may experience some moments of tranquility along the way.

The reason peace is so elusive is that it can only come from a right relationship with God, made possible only through his Son Jesus. *He is our peace!*

The one who created our hearts is the only one who can satisfy them.

I love how he's called the Prince of Peace, and Jehovah-Shalom (the LORD is Peace). We're promised that when we fill our minds with him, trust him in the dark, and keep our hearts open to communing with him, we will have peace. Supernatural peace, that far surpasses human understanding. Faith is the golden key.

And I can tell you from many years of needing his peace, that he truly does calm, comfort, soothe, reassure, and give rest!

The only way to have the peace of God is to have *peace with God.* And the good news is that it's possible!

Therefore, having been justified by faith, we have peace with God through our Lord Jesus Christ (Romans 5:1).

There is no greater peace. I hope you have it.

Some amazing peaceful truths to ponder:
Judges 6:24
Isaiah 9:6
Isaiah 26:3
Isaiah 48:22
John 14:17
Philippians 4:6–7

Survival Checklist for Seasons of Stress

There's no lack of stress in today's world, whether it's a public season or a personal season. When we're overwhelmed with the relentless pressures of just getting through the day, or surviving the deep wounds of loss or trauma, we tend to minimize the importance of taking care of ourselves. Self-care is not selfish. It's essential!

During a devastating divorce, and later the deaths of dear loved ones, and now the ongoing challenges of living in the world of PTSD, the following Survival Checklist has truly been a lifeline to me. I hope you find it helpful too.

___Pour out your heart to God.

There will be times when you come before him and have no words. Lay your petitions at his feet. Claim his promises. Take comfort in his eternal love.

___Immerse yourself in God's Word.

God's Word is true, powerful, and supernatural. And yet it is amazingly personal. His Word brings strength, hope, wisdom, and peace. Ask him to show you a special promise or word of encouragement today.

___In times of loss, put off major decisions if possible.

It's necessary to live through all four seasons, with holidays, birthdays, anniversaries, and other memories. Along with healing comes clearer thinking. Circumstances will change and so will you.

___Feel the feelings in a healthy way.

You are not responsible for feelings that come uninvited, but for what you do with them. Identify the feeling. Own it. Resist the temptation just to cover up the pain with something that feels good. Then find a healthy outlet (journaling, writing, talking, yelling, crying, running, cleaning, creating art, singing, exercising, going for a walk, playing with a pet, etc.). Letting the feelings out in a healthy way will pay off!

___Talk to someone trustworthy. Get support.

Who are the people you can share with—family, friends, pastor, counselor? Surround yourself with healthy, wise, supportive individuals. There also might be times when solitude is what you need most because you are exhausted.

___Keep your sense of humor. ☺

Scripture has taught for centuries what medical research has validated: *"A merry heart does good,* like *medicine."* (Proverbs 17:22a) Appropriate laughter is actually good for you, physically and emotionally.

___Carefully choose your sources of input.

Reading material, social media/internet, TV, movies, radio, podcasts, music, and input from people can greatly impact your well-being. Provide yourself with as much positive input as you can, and avoid negative or disturbing sources.

___Make sleep a priority.

Sleep is one of the hardest things during times of stress, but it is absolutely essential. A full night's rest, and afternoon naps when possible, will help tremendously. Sleep is our restorative companion, not a luxury.

___Fill your body with healthy things.

Your body is on a physiological battlefield. It's up to you to supply and reinforce it. Stress weakens the immune system, so anything you can do to build up your resistance will be beneficial. Do your best to get the nutrients you need, and avoid things that are depleting.

___Do some physical activity every day.

In the stress of life, time is a precious commodity, and exercise is often a low priority. Just twenty to sixty minutes a day of moving your body can increase your energy and help you think more clearly. Exercise can release endorphins, the body's natural tranquilizer and mood enhancer, and also boost the immune system and improve sleep.

___Let yourself feel special. ♥

Self-deprivation is not a virtue. During this difficult season of your life, remind yourself that you are special. Hopefully your friends and loved ones are supportive. Also, don't put off needed dental and medical care.

___Decide when to take some time off and when to be actively involved.

It may be necessary to bow out of some activities or events. Having good boundaries sometimes means saying "No." Ask yourself, *"Is this energizing and lifting me up, or is it draining me?"*

___Let go of what is beyond your control.

The future is daunting. Life feels so overwhelming! If you have done everything you can, then consciously let go. Choose to trust God to lead you through the uncertainties of tomorrow. He knows everything, and we do not. He is all powerful, and we are not. You've heard the wise saying, *"Let go and let God."*

And I like to remember that *I can let go, because he doesn't.*

___Count your blessings.

We're so focused on easing our pain and getting past our problems, that gratitude is usually not on our radar. Think of the positive things that have happened, how your needs are being met, and all we're prone to take for granted. Try to name ten things every day, and your world will brighten as you choose to give thanks.

___Trust God.

Perhaps your faith in God has been shaken a bit lately. Where has he been, and if he is good why does he allow such hard times? He never promised us a comfortable life here, and we know we all have an appointment with death. That is the whole reason he sent his Son to die for us on the cross. Then he rose again, triumphantly conquering death forever! Reach out in faith. He is worthy of your trust.

___Let time work.

As you take healthy steps of self-care each day, you will grow. Let time work for you. Let God work in you. And one day you will look back and be amazed at how He actually brought good things out of this seemingly hopeless season.

No longer merely surviving… you'll be thriving!

(~ Adapted from *Goodbye for Now* and *Formerly a Wife,* both by Welby O'Brien)

Save the Package

Remember the torture right before Christmas or a birthday of looking at all the packages and having to wait? Not public knowledge until now, but one year I couldn't stand not knowing what was in one of the boxes. So when no one was around I opened it (and rewrapped it). Ironically it wasn't the guilt that bothered me most, but rather my stressing about how I could successfully convince them all of my surprise and delight when I opened it!

Life is a continuous series of unknown circumstances—packages—that loom in front of us, resulting in ongoing battles with anxiety.

We're driven to figure it all out in advance, enslaved to the delusion that once we solve this particular challenge, we'll be done. (And will have executed it flawlessly, of course!) Sound familiar? 😉 The perplexing problem packages cannot wait—they must be opened now! And my mind *must work on it 24/7* until I feel more in control.

When we tear open the "package" before its intended time, not only do we lose out on the beauty of living in the present moment, but we also forfeit the joy of anticipation, as well as the strength and faith that grow from waiting and trusting.

God never intended us to be in bondage to hurry or worry, neither of which are good for us. What if we were to change our mindset and visualize the object of our anxiety not as an enemy to conquer, but as a *gift*? A gift from God to be opened in His timing...and no sooner.

The image of packages helps minimize the negative scenarios we so readily contrive, which ironically rarely come to pass.

So how do we change our mindset? What helps me most is filling my mind with a scriptural game plan. This passage that says it all is an excerpt from Paul's letter written from a very unpleasant prison cell.

> **The Lord *is* at hand** (the whole reason we don't have to be anxious!).
>
> **Be anxious for nothing** (not even just a few things?), **but in everything by prayer and supplication, with thanksgiving** (seems counterintuitive, but in spite of the challenges there is plenty we can be grateful for), **let your requests be made known to God** (take the time and talk honestly with Him). **And the peace of God** (which we so desperately need!), **which surpasses all understanding** (it won't be logical to have peace in the middle of unresolved issues so don't try to figure God out), **will guard your hearts and your minds through Christ Jesus** (sounds soothingly safe to me)**.** (Philippians 4:5b–7, thoughts in parentheses are mine)

So when I find my mind trapped in the vicious cycle of nonstop problem solving, I need to say, *"This can wait. Save the package."* And then pray, "Lord, please give me what I need when I need it, and show me what to do and when to do it."

Then I'll wiggle my toes (for grounding), breathe, smile, and give thanks for the many *blessings I have right now!* 🙂

Be Quieted (with His Love)

Life is noisy! Noise is disturbing. Distressing. Disconcerting. Ever notice that when it suddenly becomes quiet, you feel relieved? Calmed. Quieted.

God never intended for us to be bombarded with endless blare, and all its accompanying high-decibel distress. But since much of life is cranked up with constant clamor, can we find the quietness we so desperately crave?

We're told in Zephaniah 3:17 that *"He will quiet you with His love."* Nice verse. But *what* does it mean and *how* will he do it?

In pondering this, it struck me that God's love does not exist in a vacuum. It's not merely a warm fuzzy concept. His love is demonstrated physically and practically, in the very world we inhabit, and in the seemingly senseless circumstances we experience. So his quieting would also be manifested in a tangible way. Both on his part and on ours.

As I see it, the disturbing noise of life bombards us in two ways: pain and pressure.

We all have suffered with pain, feeling both physical and emotional pain (grief, fear, remorse, etc.). God's quieting love answers and soothes our pain when we meet him by faith at the cross of his Son. A very physical demonstration of his quieting love. And because his love is eternal, it supersedes everything else that will eventually come to an end, including all pain.

Another distressing noise in our lives that needs quieting is pressure. Feeling harried, stressed, overwhelmed. The ceaseless clamor of just getting through the day. And in this age of nonstop communication, solitude is a lost treasure.

For me, to receive God's quieting love in a real way, I need to do something physical. Mary got it right. While her sister was stressing about housework, Mary sat down—took a little time out from the stress. She purposely let herself *be quieted* in the presence of the Lord.

She let him love her. She listened to him. And that silenced the noise.

What do you need that will quiet you long enough to grasp the extent his love? For you? When we push the mute button and pause briefly to engage our physical senses in a calming way, we can be quieted. Maybe it's a cozy chair, herbal tea, essential oils, soothing music, or a scenic photo. Be still. Listen. Hear his Word. What is he saying to you?

When we sit still and listen to his love, the noise of life fades.

And after a little time out, when we resume our tasks, we can do so with a calmer, deeper grasp of His love, and a glimpse of where that love will carry us in the days, years, and eternity ahead. ♥

"That you may be able to comprehend with all the saints what *is* the width and length and depth and height—to know the love of Christ which passes knowledge; that you may be filled with all the fullness of God." (Ephesians 3:18–19)

CHAPTER THIRTEEN

Caregiver Kudos

Prayer:

Thank you, Lord, that you promise to give us what we need when we need it. Please help us be faithful to you, as we rely on your strength for this day.

Holding On to Your Joy: Can Joy and PTSD Coexist?

I was always a bubbly person, with a laugh ready to rip at any moment. But the more time I spent in the world of PTSD as a trauma survivor and a caregiver, the more I noticed my joy dwindling.

Whether you care for someone with PTSD or other challenges, giving 24/7 can take its toll.

They say that those of us who love our PTSD survivors are prone to acquiring second-hand PTSD. Whether first- or second-hand trauma, being in survival mode 24/7 is a challenge that can overpower a joyful light heart.

Is it possible for joy and caregiving to coexist? Is it possible for joy and PTSD to coexist?

Recently a friend shared that she heard a loud battle cry from the bedroom! Running to see what was wrong, she stopped in the doorway, watching her husband swinging his shorts violently around the room. "There's a bug in here!" he yelled. He whacked and whipped and ran around trying to smack that bug.

Of course, she laughed. And for most people, it would have been funny. But he was triggered, and to him, it was not a humorous occasion.

Eventually, after he calmed down, they were able to chuckle a little. (Last I heard the bug is still at large). But the incident reminds me that first, we need to be respectful of their triggers and not laugh at them if they are not laughing themselves. And second, we should be free to enjoy *our joy,* even if we must leave the room to do so considerately.

We tend to match, or take on, their downward moods and negativity, and it requires a conscious effort to hold on to our own joy when it is not being shared. (In my book, *Love Our Vets: Restoring Hope for Families of Veterans with PTSD,* I address a multitude of issues unique to loved ones of those battling PTSD.)

I'm finally realizing that it's okay to be happy! Scripture is filled with reminders to rejoice and be glad. And with Jesus, his joy can outshine the darkest moments.

The following are some ideas that have helped many of us, and I can affirm *it is possible for joy and PTSD to coexist.* 🙂

- Start the day looking for blessings and surprises.
- Minimize sources of negativity (news, social media, certain people, etc.).
- Actively express gratitude. There's always something to be grateful for.
- Remember to differentiate between their well-being and yours. You are *not them.*
- Remind yourself that you are not responsible for their feelings and reactions.
- Self-care is paramount: time alone, listening to relaxing music, getting fresh air, walking or other exercise, reading a book, etc. Try to nurture all five senses.
- Cultivate a joyful mindset. Choose to think about things that are happy, uplifting, positive, and extinguish the negative thoughts. Studies show that whatever our brain thinks about the most is what it will crave and cultivate.

- Smile all the time! 🙂 This will also positively impact your brain and mood. I put smiley faces all around the house to remind me.
- Seek friends and supporters who lift you up and bring you joy, hopefully mutual.
- Play with your dog or cat as much as you can. Or enjoy someone else's whenever you get the chance.
- Make a list of what you love doing, and do something every day: sing and dance in the kitchen, go to the drag races, grow a little garden, paint, do crafts or fun projects, watch something hilarious, play an instrument, try a new recipe, go for a scenic drive, read a great book, clean out a drawer or closet, go out to eat with friends, treat yourself to fresh flowers, take pictures, send upbeat greeting cards or messages, start a collection of memes that make you laugh, etc.
- Laugh freely by yourself when you can. Make silly faces and smile in the mirror. Be goofy and enjoy it!
- Keep a joy journal, a happy log. Write down everything during the day that makes you happy and that you are thankful for. Read it over when you need a pick-me-up!
- Talk to God. Soak up scripture and sing praises to him! Truly a game changer for me and so many!
- Finally, *be* the joy in someone else's life, even if it's just a smile.

Although we can't change others, we can choose to brighten our own lives on this journey. ♥

"The joy of the Lord is your strength." (Nehemiah 8:10)

Faithful Over a Few Things

Have you ever dreamed of doing something really great for God? To impact many lives, and make a difference in this world? Just the awesomeness of knowing your life really mattered? And you secretly wish: "If only I had a servant who could do all the menial stuff, then I could be free to do the really important things for God"?

I confess that I've had it upside down all this time! I assumed that bigger is always better, and our goal is always more. (Oops.)

I did a double take listening again to what Jesus said about the day we stand before him. The master entrusted each person with something different, along with a unique job to do. Then when he came back, the one who did what he told him to do received a warm, joyful welcome!

His lord said to him, **"Well *done*, good and faithful servant;** you were faithful over a few things, I will make you ruler over many things. Enter into the joy of your lord." (Mathew 25:21)

Serving the Lord can be challenging and also exciting. But we have to guard against equating the thrill of the work with its true value. Or to assume earthly numbers have parallel significance in Heaven. *That one person who needs us today is far more important than we realize!* And our faithfulness in doing those seemingly menial tasks that consume our days is pleasing to the Lord.

Rather than asking, *"How much am I doing for God?"* perhaps we should be asking ourselves:

How am I doing with the people God has put in my life and under my care, and the responsibilities he has entrusted to me?

Here's what I'm trying to remember:

1. God doesn't need me to do stuff for him; he wants to work through me!

2. God doesn't tell us to do a lot and to do it perfectly; he tells us to be faithful with what he has given us to do.

3. When we seek the Lord and his will with all our heart, he will give us what we need when we need it, to do what he wants when he wants.

So throughout the day whenever we catch ourselves grumbling, or dreaming about one day doing something really important for God, ask him to help us be "faithful over a few."

Hard to imagine anything more rewarding than to hear my master say, "Well done, good and faithful servant."

Lord, please help me be faithful in the few things you have for me today, and keep my eyes on the joy that awaits! ♥

The Nozzle

I struggle a lot with wanting to help others, and really make an eternal difference in this world for the Lord. Sound noble? Read on. 😉

The hard part is the constant battle to resist pride (when things go well and I can see fruit), and the opposite extreme of self-imposed pressure and anxiety (when I can't see fruit and think I should be doing more.)

Pretty sure this is not the way the Lord set things up. So in our desire to walk in his will for our lives, how do we find that elusive ideal middle ground between pride ("Yay… look what I did!") and pressure ("Is that all you can do?")?

On a recent hot summer evening while watering the thirsty yard with the hose, I noticed the shiny brass nozzle I held. Wow! It hit me! The nozzle is an important tool for dissemination, but the real source of life is *the water itself.* No room for nozzle pride.

Likewise, it is *the water itself* that goes out to bear the fruit. The results are not up to the nozzle. No room for nozzle fear or anxiety.

He is the Water.

Just show up and let the Water flow out.

And as we continue to seek his direction and leading, discovering what is important to God, there is a beautiful freedom and authenticity that begins to flow out through us. Maybe it is actually not social media stats that really matter. (What???!)

Maybe it's that one person who crosses your path today whom you can encourage . . . perhaps without even realizing it. Or maybe someone actually living in your home . . . scary, huh?

My prayer is to be the very best nozzle I can be and let him do the rest. I hope you feel watered today.

" . . . He who believes in Me, as the Scripture has said, out of his heart will flow rivers of living water."
~Jesus (John 7:38)

Three Ways to Celebrate Love with or Without a Valentine

Not everyone loves Valentine's Day. Especially if your Valentine is gone or has changed. My dear friend lost her beloved husband *on* Valentine's Day.

Divorce, separation, death, and PTSD can overwhelm the wounded heart with grief, pain, and loneliness, which only intensifies during a holiday where others are celebrating love that for you is now a mere memory.

I've personally known the devastation of abandonment, loss, heartbreak, and trauma. And I've also been blessed with true fulfilling love later in life . . . despite the PTSD.

I had to walk through the challenges and victories of progressing one painful step at a time—from barely surviving to really living. Those first few steps can be the hardest.

Whether this is a good time or a deep valley, we can always celebrate love. Contrary to what many assume, love is not merely a warm fuzzy feeling. *True love takes action!*

The following are three actions that have helped me over the years, not just on Valentine's Day, but also for the ups and downs of everyday life.

1. Love Yourself ♥

Self-care is so much more than manicures, massages, and movies. Try incorporating a self-scan into your daily routine. Stop. (Really.) Ask, "What do I need right now?" Then take care of that need.

Consider your spiritual needs (such as listening to God and pouring out your heart to him), your physical needs (such as getting enough sleep, nutrients, and regular exercise), and your emotional needs (such as processing the feelings in a healthy way, and surrounding yourself with good support).

Self-care is not a luxury, but a lifeline. And when we take care of ourselves, those around us will also benefit.

2. Love Someone Else ♥

When I'm struggling, one of the best things I can do is reach out to someone else who may be hurting. Not only does it take my mind off myself, but it's also a blessing to the other person.

Who do you know that could use some encouragement today? Pray for them. Maybe take them a gift basket, or give them a call or email. Or send a card in the mail (remember how to do that?). 😉

Love in action will also help put our own pain in perspective.

3. Love God and Let Him Love You ♥

This is truly the supreme love to celebrate! Nothing on this earth can ever come close to the joy and peace that a relationship with God offers. God's all surpassing grace was expressed through the suffering and death of his Son on the cross . . . for us who deserve nothing but eternal separation from him.

This love we can celebrate any time . . . now and throughout eternity.

And we can rest assured that he will never leave, and he will never change. Not even the most amazing earthly Valentine could ever come close.

I hope you are able to celebrate all three of these loves. Every day! ♥

Jesus said to him, "'You shall love the Lord your God with all your heart, with all your soul, and with all your mind.'

This is *the* first and great commandment. And *the* second *is* like it: 'You shall love your neighbor as yourself.' . . . " (Matthew 22:37–39)

Hope for Caregivers

Feeling alone, overwhelmed, helpless, weary, abandoned, hopeless, angry, depressed, or confused? Take a slow deep breath and give yourself a hug. You are normal!

Most of us who love and care for someone else have huge hearts. And it seems like the harder we try to fix things or understand them, the more frustrated we get! That is why many loved ones either burn out or just throw in the towel and walk away.

Learning about—and accepting my limitations (and failures)—has been an ongoing process. Let me share a few things that have been helpful to me on my own journey. Hope you find them helpful as well.

- I cannot always help the one I love.
- I cannot make others understand.
- I cannot help everyone.
- I cannot fix the world, or any person.
- I cannot stop pain and injustice.
- I cannot maintain a perfect relationship or an ideal home.
- I cannot always have a great day.

But...

- I *can* love someone who needs me.
- I *can* connect with others who understand.
- I *can* offer encouragement to others.
- I *can* listen to someone in need.
- I *can* help spread awareness.
- I *can* keep on learning and growing.
- I *can* ask the Lord for strength and grace.

- I *can* take care of me.

It's totally okay to have a meltdown, to cry, to pray, to reach out to someone who is good for us, and to laugh at ourselves when we can. Tomorrow is always another day.

Let's do what we tell our loved ones: *"Just do the best you can. And that is okay!"* ♥

I can do all things through Christ who strengthens me. (Philippians 4:13)

CHAPTER FOURTEEN

Trauma Care

Prayer:

Dear Lord, thank you that sometimes it's in our darkest moments that we find you to be the true treasure of our faith. Help us trust your promises that you know, you care, and you are here.

The Three Most Neglected Areas of Self-Care During Trauma, Stress, and Loss

Struggling with trauma, stress, or loss? Grief? Anxiety? Is hope merely an elusive dream? When thrust into survival mode, self-preservation dominates all we think and do. The mandate is *do whatever it takes to survive!* Get through alive.

Self-care, on the other hand, is considered just a luxury, a thing of the past.

Or could it potentially be even more crucial in the long run than basic self-preservation?

Even with a degree in counseling, and decades of ministering to others, I too have personally experienced grief, loss, and trauma. I'm also the grateful wife of an amazing combat veteran who battles PTSD. And as each day passes, I suspect that many people around the world are also feeling as if they are caught in a fight, flight, or freeze survival mode.

I've learned that post-traumatic stress disorder (PTSD) can result from exposure to a traumatic or life-threatening experience, and when the whole person gets permanently programmed into emergency survival mode, it affects them and their loved ones for the rest of their lives. (Find more information and resources at www.LoveOurVets.org and in my book, *Love Our Vets: Restoring Hope for Families of Veterans with PTSD).* ♥

Self-preservation is an instinct granted by God to much of His creation. But is there more? Are we destined to be consumed with the challenges of merely surviving, or can this fundamental self-preservation be enhanced and enriched?

The good news is that our Creator has gifted us with the privilege of making choices. Beyond mere instinct lies the rich realm of self-care.

Not a luxury, but perhaps of greater long-term value than simply surviving: *we have the option of thriving!*

And emerging on the other side of each challenging season with far more than we had when we entered it.

My wake-up call came one spring morning in the kitchen after a restless disturbing night. I was tired, depressed, and felt like I was shriveling up inside. Then I looked out the window at the rising sun, budding trees, and blooming tulips. It was as if they said, "You too can come alive and thrive in this season!"

That was the moment I chose to not just survive, but to thrive!

So I found a favorite Christmas CD, and before I knew it, I was singing and dancing in the kitchen! I had begun to reclaim my joy and peace.

It took a conscious effort to activate the self-care I desperately needed. But the payoff has been so rewarding! The following are three areas—with some specific suggestions for starters—that many of us tend to neglect when we are in survival mode.

1. Emotional Care

___ Process your feelings in a healthy way (journaling, talking, crying . . .)

___ Set boundaries when needed

___ Stay connected to good people
___ Take a break from negative social media and news
___ Keep your sense of humor

2. Spiritual Care

___ Soak up scripture
___ Fill your mind with other uplifting truths
___ Pour out your heart to God in prayer
___ Be still . . . and listen
___ Thank the Lord for the blessings you do have

3. Physical Care

___ Nurture yourself via all five senses
___ Allow yourself plenty of sleep and rest
___ Continue necessary medical care
___ Focus on quality nutrition
___ Get regular exercise and fresh air

These steps will not only prove to be a lifeline in times of crisis, but they are valuable habits to incorporate in everyday life. When we intentionally cultivate our relationship with the Lord, and take care of ourselves in many other ways, we actually grow. We learn. We benefit.

And we emerge stronger and more resilient than we would have if we just picked up where we left off.

The best news of all is that when we choose to trust our Creator and Savior by receiving his gift of salvation and eternal life, he will preserve us and care for us forever.

One day, as we look back, I think there will be a marked difference between those who merely survived instinctively and those who chose to thrive intentionally. I hope to be part of that victory! 

"Thanks be to God, who gives us the victory through our Lord Jesus Christ." (1 Corinthians 15:57)

Your Name Here

Would it blow you away to find out that God has a special book filled with the names of those who honor Him, and meditate on His name?

> **"Those who feared the LORD spoke to one another, and the LORD listened and heard. So a book of remembrance was written before Him of those who fear the LORD and who meditate on His name."** (Malachi 3:16)

Amazing! In my recent ongoing recovery from a serious illness (thank the Lord I am doing so much better!), one thing I started doing was filling my mind with the names of the Lord. Especially in the lonely waking moments of the night.

I've spent much of my life trying to get to sleep or get back to sleep over the years. Ugh. But now, what I do (it took time and commitment) is when I start to wake up, I immediately say, "Jesus." Or "Prince of Peace." Or "My Good Shepherd" . . . etc. I love it! I feel so close to the Lord whenever I meditate on his name.

It has transformed restless nights to be so much more peaceful and joyful, which carries over to the next day. 😆

I did a search for the names of God in the Bible and found a pretty good list to meditate on (night or day.) You can do the same. One idea is to make a list of thirty-one of your favorite names of God and focus on one name for each day of the month. Or have a few of your personal favorites to enjoy dwelling on regularly. Some of mine are:

Jehovah "I AM THAT I AM"

El-Shaddai (God Almighty)
Creator
Jehovah-Shalom (God is Peace)
Jehovah-Jireh (God Who Provides)
Jehovah-Rapha (God Who Heals)
God of Angel Armies
Comforter
Abba Father
Wonderful Counselor
Emmanuel – God with Us
King of Kings and Lord of Lords
Jeshua/Jesus (Jehovah is Salvation)

I also have incorporated some very helpful neuroplasticity protocols, which have been key to my healing. *Whatever we choose to think about, that part of our brain will grow.* If we're inclined toward negativity, and choose to think and talk about how terrible things are, our brain and heart will seek more of that to feed on.

But, if we choose to fill our minds and hearts with uplifting, peaceful, and joyful truths, our brains will gradually want more and more, and will eventually automatically be inclined toward those happy thoughts and feelings. I know—it has happened to me! 😆

The other part I realized is that *what we choose to talk about* will also impact the development of our neural pathways. So I've also learned that talking with others about the Lord really brings me joy, and perspective, and hope. (And I've chosen to *not* talk about controversial news issues at all. It's wonderful!)

I encourage you to give it a try. So simple, really. Nothing fancy.

Just think about the Lord, especially his name, and talk with each other about him.

Then watch for new blessings, including your name in God's special book.

Reflections from My Recent Valley of the Shadow

(Written in 2016)

We've heard it said that when everything else is taken away, then we find that God is all we really need. I always believed that but never had a chance to experience it. Until the last few weeks.

Rushed to the hospital deathly ill, twice in eight days, I lost everything. The first was an emergency appendectomy, just in the nick of time. That was followed days later by a deadly C.diff infection, which once again I almost did not make it through.

Instantaneously, I was stripped of all comforts, and many other things that are essential for survival. For days, I was not allowed to drink, eat, sleep, leave my room, or touch my loving husband, to name a few. Instead, I was poked, pierced, probed, cut on, chained to an IV, diagnostically irradiated repeatedly, and I could barely function. I was too sick to even turn on the TV.

I was so deep in the valley that I could barely cry; but when I did, it felt so good to weep. Trauma—and PTSD—has an even deeper meaning for me now than ever before.

Then, my own body refused to let me eat for three weeks due to the medication that was saving my life, and I found myself literally starving to death.

The prayers of so many dear people touched my heart—and I know God heard them. The love of my precious husband held me up. But what will probably change me forever were the dark, lonely, frightening times when I was alone. I had nothing. All that was so important to me the day before this all began had vanished. It was all meaningless.

Nothing mattered except surviving. Yet surprisingly, even that paled in comparison to knowing that the Lord was there with me. In my darkness, the light of hope that Heaven—and all he has said—really is true. We have no other hope but him—and what a blessed hope that is!

Yet, as I look back, I feel convicted of my lack of faith in many of the dark moments. He seemed so far away at times. Why did he not answer me and fix me? Now I realize that he *was* there, and I *did* trust him.

The treasure of faith is not how *much* I have—measured by how little I am afraid, or struggle, or wrestle, or have questions—but rather *who* is the object of my faith.

The tiniest frailest line will connect me with him—and that is all I need. That faith pleases him, and that teeny bit of faith is what has the eternal value. With or without the fear and doubts.

He was with me. In my pain and fear and trauma. *And every time I thought I couldn't take any more, he carried me a little further.* ♥

What a comfort to have so many scripture verses come to mind—all through the day, and the seemingly endless nights. How very precious it is to be so close to him, my Good Shepherd. And Jesus is no stranger to pain and rejection and fear and trauma.

My prayer through it all was that nothing would be wasted. I wanted to find the treasures along the way and not forget them after it was all behind me. I wanted to leave the hospital a changed person.

So here I sit, writing this down as I recover and begin to rebuild, because I know my nature will be to just move forward without looking back. If I had to sum it up, the three greatest treasures I have gained are:

1. **Greater compassion for the sick and disabled.**
2. **Greater appreciation for all the blessings of life we so easily take for granted.**
3. **Confirmation that God and our relationship with him through Jesus is all we need; and in the long run nothing else matters.**

Please remind me of this when I start to complain that the food isn't to my liking, or the traffic is jammed, or I have a headache, or I wish I had a nicer house, or I feel fat.

It's just good to be alive and be able to praise the Lord for all his blessings!

And if he chooses to take them away for a while again, then I know he will be with me; and that is all I really need. Because all I really need he has already prepared for me—and in his perfect timing, he will come get me to take me where I will always be with him. And never ever again be sick. Or hungry. Or thirsty. Or in pain. Or afraid.

And that solid hope keeps us going in the dark valleys.

Going to go eat now. And oh so gratefully! And then I will hold my precious husband tightly . . . oh so gratefully! And then I will sleep well tonight knowing whose hands I am in. ♥

He Himself has said, "I will never leave you nor forsake you."

So we may boldly say: "The LORD is my helper; I will not fear." (Hebrews 13:5-6)

Stressed Around the Holidays? Here's Hope!

Winter is off to a brutal start this time of year. And just the mention of the holidays and the Christmas season can send chills up our spines! Along with guilt because this should be "the most wonderful time of the year" . . . or so they say.

Add to that the imposed assumption that people of faith should not get stressed about anything, let alone one of our most quintessential days of celebration!

Unfortunately, we are human. Christians or not, this can be a very hard time for many. Cold stormy weather, darkness, power outages, holiday hoopla, excessive special events, family stresses, increased financial pressures, painful memories, extra obligations, overloaded schedules, junk food galore, lack of exercise, more crowds, less space, emotional upheavals, etc.

I received a desperate message from a young mother reeling from a recent divorce:

"There's no way I am going to make it through this year!"

We all know the feeling! Whether we're ready to pull out our hair, or in the depths of despair and ready to end it all, none of this seasonal stress is helpful to anyone. Especially those who are suffering. You may be homeless, or have lost a loved one, or are battling cancer, or are a PTSD survivor . . . to name a few. And the ripple effect of the stress deeply impacts all those close to us as well.

So since we can't fast-forward to spring, how do we best make it through these colder, busier, darker, more difficult days?

Personally, to name a few challenges, I've survived winter during divorce, during grief, during life-threatening illness, during financial downturns, and as a first- and second-hand PTSD survivor.

Knowing the Lord and leaning heavily on his promises in the cold and darkness has been my lifeline.

But even then, the stresses and challenges still wage war against all of us.

Here are a few things that have helped me:

1. Be aware of your triggers.

What circumstances (and people) cause your stress to increase? Learn to recognize your symptoms as well as what triggers them.

2. Stay tuned to your body's warning signals.

Listen to your body. Learn to trust it. Does that headache, or indigestion, or grinding teeth mean anything? In order to survive, we need to be aware of our needs and be able to communicate them *(ideally, before we have a meltdown).*

3. Do all you can to stay safe and healthy.

Each of us is a choice maker. Although illness, PTSD, grief and stress can be tyrannical at times, ultimately, we have the power to choose what's best for us in the long run. And not giving in to destructive behaviors will pay off, not only for us but for those we love.

4. Remember you can't keep everyone happy.

Surprise! (I'm just now learning this!) Plan to disappoint a few people if necessary in order to save your own sanity.

Do try, however, to be polite if possible. Learning to say, "No, thank you," graciously comes with practice.

5. Be good to you.

Take time to do what you need and want. This is no longer a luxury but a necessity. I call it my "Survival Checklist" . . . found in my books, *Formerly A Wife* and *Goodbye for Now.* And for caregivers and loved ones, *Love Our Vets: Restoring Hope for Families of Veterans with PTSD* devotes the entire middle section to caring for our own needs.

Do you even know what you really *need?* Perhaps you need a light box to perk up the dark days, your favorite music, a new winter activity/sport, tastier cuisine, afternoon naps, indoor exercise, a canine companion, etc. You are worth it!

6. Surround yourself with good support and call for extra help if needed.

Who are the people who are helpful (not the leech type)? Reach out to those who are supportive. *How did we swallow the lie that toughing it out alone is more heroic?*

God designed us to need him first, and each other second. The courage to reach out for help when needed is truly admirable! Call a friend or someone you know who cares. There are people waiting to talk with you.

Always feel free to call the National Crisis Hotline: 988

7. Cherish the beautiful moments.

No matter how much craziness this life throws at us, there is always something for which to be grateful. Don't forget to pause during the chaos to give thanks for all the blessings you do have.

A good place to start is Christmas itself, and *who* we are celebrating! ♥

There's no need to dread the days ahead. Stay connected with God, and with those who are good for you, and take care of you. One day—one moment—at a time.

It will be spring before you know it! (And then we will probably be moaning about the heat, the need to pull weeds, and sunburn!) 😉

Who Cares?

Don't know why I couldn't have figured out that going down a flight of cement stairs with untied shoelaces was a bad idea. I guess at age six you don't know everything yet. 😉

So, emerging with several goose egg bumps on my head, I needed comfort. Thankfully, my mother was there. She knew what had happened, she cared (probably in pain herself), and most of all, she was there. With me. To comfort me in her arms.

Since then, I have learned to tie my shoes, and also learned that *comfort is not the removal of pain, but it is knowing that everything is going to be all right.*

For some strange reason, pain is not so bad when someone is there to hold us.

Most people experience some level of pain, stress, anxiety, or discomfort in life. I often wonder why God allows pain, knowing that he is quite capable of removing it. Is it possible that there is something ultimately better than being without pain?

The good news is that we don't have to understand it all. In fact, he never tells us to figure things out. Wow. He does, however, frequently tell us to trust him. Hmmmm. To draw close to him, the God of all comfort.

As I say in the book *Goodbye for Now,* **comfort is not the removal of pain, but it is knowing that with the Lord everything is going to be all right.** 💜

Recently, struggling with a very perplexing question in my life, I came across Psalms 142–145 (written by a man who knew well the pain and trauma and fears of life.) At the heart of my frustration (okay, meltdown) was the complaint that *no one understood what I was going through.*

The feeling of aloneness was agonizing. Thankfully, in my case there are precious people who care very much; but even then, no other person can personally experience and share the depths of your own pain. *With one exception.*

In reading these Psalms, three facts came leaping off the page:

He knows. He cares. He is here.

Realizing that the God of all comfort—Jesus—the one who died for me, *knows*, I can relax.

He *cares*; I can rest.

He *is here*; I can lean on him as he wraps me in his everlasting arms.

Everything is going to be all right. ♥

Can You Get "Untriggered"? A GPS for PTSD

Being seriously ill is no fun. Toss in a good dose of PTSD and you've got the perfect storm! My husband had been sick for a while and suddenly took a downward turn—right before bedtime—crumpled over, high fever, and feeling like he was on death's door. I hadn't been feeling well either, and we were both desperate for sleep.

"I don't know what to do! Do I go to bed, or to the VA ER? I don't know what to do!" he kept repeating. He was triggered!

Then I panicked. It would kill me to stay up all night in the ER with him. I needed my strength to take care of him. And what if we went there, and they wouldn't see him and just sent him home again?

We were both triggered! There was no answer. No solution. And no one to help.

I just wanted to run! Far away. Or *do something!* But what? I felt like my body and mind were spinning out of control.

Then I chose to get alone, sit in my comfy chair, and pray. Breathe.

Breathe some more.

Let myself relax in my "safe and happy place" for as long as it took.

After about fifteen minutes, I could feel myself coming back together again. Then (and only then) did I get an idea. I could call the ER and see what they suggested. What an answer to prayer! It was *so* clear. And it was the answer. They said, "Yes, come now."

Willing—at that point—to be up all night, I offered to take him. He was able to think clearly now, had a burst of energy, and to my relief he insisted on driving himself. We prayed together and had a good hug. And I cried when he left.

He ended up staying most of the night there, and came home with some medication for pneumonia. It was a good thing that he went! And guess what? I slept like a baby all night! Now that was another miracle.

Thankfully he is doing so much better now, and I've had time to reflect on the whole thing. So to be better prepared for next time (yup . . . there *will* be a next time), what is my takeaway?

Three things (remember **GPS—Grounding, Prayer, Support)**:

1. Grounding

Discover what works for you. There are lots of techniques to experiment with. If you haven't tried any, an internet search for "grounding techniques" will offer plenty of options. Or ask others what helps them. Taking steps toward getting grounded is something we all can do.

2. Prayer

Here's where God fits in . . . connecting us to a Higher Power when we most need it.

When we get triggered, our brains are stuck in emergency response mode, and we can't see our way out. We feel so alone. So helpless. I'm not advocating "religion" per se, but rather a *relationship with him,* which offers help and hope.

3. Support

As I remind us in my book, *Love Our Vets: Restoring Hope for Families of Veterans with PTSD*, connecting with others is a vital lifeline. Only those living with PTSD themselves can truly grasp the overwhelming challenges 24/7. 365. Local groups or online, or even a "battle buddy" within reach will be a great help, not just in the hard times but in between as well.

Now I've got a GPS ready to go for the next perfect storm. In the meantime, I'm gonna go give my wonderful husband a big hug. 🙂

CHAPTER FIFTEEN

Fresh Starts

Prayer:

Dear Lord, thank you that every morning is a fresh start on our journey with you. Please help us live by faith today, knowing that what matters most is where we are going with you.

No Regrets

One of my least favorite things is New Year's resolutions. "What do you need to change?" How depressing to come off a month-long holiday high, only to make a list of things you need to fix—most of which are just plain no fun!

And to make matters worse, most of us fail miserably at following through with those changes we thought we *needed* to make at the beginning of the year. So I decided to ask myself a different question at the beginning of each new year.

At the end of this year as I look back on my life, what do I want to be able to say?

All our good intentions don't have to be cast aside. It is wise to maintain a healthy weight, avoid addictive behaviors, pay off debts, do well in school, etc. *But, at the end of the year, or even more importantly at the end of my life, what will matter most?*

When I stand before the Lord, I doubt he will say, "I am so impressed! You passed up the cheeseburgers and bon bons, paid off most of your credit cards, and your sock drawer was impeccable!"

Ultimately, I want to have no regrets. But what is my standard for that? About what, specifically, do I want to have no regrets? After spending some time wrestling with this question, I finally came up with what to me is—and will be—the most crucial way to spend my life.

And knowing no better authority on what is truly important, I am taking my cues from the words of Jesus:

You shall love the LORD your God with all your heart, with all your soul, and with all your mind. This is the first and great commandment. And the second is like it: You shall love your neighbor as yourself. (Matthew 22:37–39)

For me, having no regrets means desiring to actually live out these two commands—all through the day, every day.

At the end of the year, and the end of my life, I want to know that God truly has been my first love, not only in my thoughts but in my actions. And that I have been a channel of his love to all those around me, beginning at home.

I hope we can all encourage each other to continue to walk by faith, to cling to what matters ultimately, and to let go of what does not.

In the meantime, I'm still going to clean out my sock drawer.

Can You Hear Me?

I don't plan to make any more New Year's resolutions except to eat more, spend more, and laugh more! Fun, huh? 🙂

More importantly, with each passing year, I want to say I know the Lord more. I love the idea of getting a head start on eternity, and truly enjoying a deep and intimate journey with God and his Son Jesus Christ—in the ups and downs of this life.

So, how do I know him more? In any relationship, you get to know someone by spending time with them and by listening to them. Prayer is good, but usually I do the talking.

When was the last time I listened to God and actually heard Him?

If God wanted to say something to me, would I hear him? Here are a few questions to consider:

- If God wanted to say something to me through a glorious sunset, would I notice?
- If God wanted to say something to me through my friends, would they be good channels of his voice?
- If God wanted to say something to me through social media, would I hear him?
- If God wanted to say something to me in my wakefulness at night, would my mind be free to hear him?
- If God wanted to say something to me in the middle of my pain, would my heart be open to him?
- If God wanted to say something to me through his written Word, do I sit still long enough to hear?

- If God wanted to say something to me from his Word by memory, would there be enough there to hear?
- If God wanted to have me all to himself at some point in my busy day, would he find me with a listening heart?

I hope you also long to hear God speak to you. What a thrill that he's made it possible to know him, the one who quiets us with his love, and rejoices over us with singing! ♥ (Zephaniah 3:17, paraphrase)

"My sheep hear My voice, and I know them."
~Jesus (John 10:27)

Sing the Scriptures!

We know that faith comes by hearing the Word of God. And most of us wish we knew more scripture by memory. But there's no easy or fun way to do that...or is there?

On the heels of my long difficult healing journey, I discovered a fun and powerful way to immerse myself in God's living Word. I've never been so happy and peaceful!

We can actually program our brains to sing God's Word!

I made a short video showing how it works. Great for all ages! And you can call it *The Song Game* if you want.

You'll surprise yourself by singing scripture when you least expect it, and when you need it most.

Take a quick look at my YouTube video to see how it works:

https://youtu.be/dyzzNr5s1Cw

Here is a website with a great list of amazing simple scriptures I've found that work well with this pattern:
https://welbyo.com/2023/07/amazing-simple-scriptures-to-song/

What an uplifting way to start each day! 🙂

GPS for Life

Isn't it great that we don't need our brains anymore when we drive? (Map? What's that?) I only wish that we could get a GPS that told us what direction to go, which way to turn, and what decisions to make in our daily lives.

God offers that service—for free! Proverbs 3:5-6 tell us to "Trust in the Lord with all your heart, and lean not on your own understanding; In all your ways acknowledge Him, And He shall direct your paths."

When we activate a GPS (Global Positioning System), it is only beneficial if we do three things. These same three things help us with God's directions:

Connect, listen, and follow.

1. In order to "activate" God's blessings, we must connect in a personal relationship with God through Jesus Christ, and seek him. *Do we want him and his ways?*

2. We have to listen to what the device tells us, or read the directions. The same is true when seeking direction from God. *Am I open to hearing what he wants for me as he speaks to me through the Bible?*

3. It does no good to connect and hear if we don't actually follow the directions. *Am I doing what I know he wants me to do right now?*

He promises to direct our paths when we seek him and trust him, and do not rely solely on our limited perspective. Like a GPS satellite system, God sees the whole picture.

And although the ride may seem rough at times, *he is the only reliable one who will get us safely to our final destination.*

Ultimately, the only thing that matters is where we end up and who we are with. ♥

First Love

Zoom back in time to your first kiss, probably your first love. Wow! You were twitterpated. Had butterflies. Couldn't eat. That love permeated and consumed every bit of you. Looking back, he or she was probably just a pimply faced teenager, but you were in love and that was all that mattered!

Whether puppy love or genuine love-of-your-life love, nothing surpasses the ecstasy of first love.

Can you recall the beginning of your love relationship with the Lord? How did you feel and act? It's intriguing to note that in all of God's relationships with man since time began **the most important thing he wants from us is to love him** (Matthew 22:37, paraphrase). He beckons us to return to our first love (Revelation 2, paraphrase).

Can you recapture that pinnacle of closeness, the wholehearted oneness with your Creator and Savior? Perhaps you've never known that yet. Now is a great time to start! He is always there beckoning us to believe, receive, and love him.

God does not expect us to conjure up mushy feelings from nowhere. But instead to *live the love* we profess. When we once thrilled at the pinnacle of passion, the height of our first love, what did we do?

Perhaps the list looked something like this:

- He/she is the last thought on my mind before I go to sleep and the first thing when I awake
- I want to be with him/her all the time
- I love talking to him/her
- I love listening to him/her
- I love talking about him/her
- I have reminders of him/her everywhere

- I love making him/her happy
- Can't get enough of those love songs!
- I love remembering all things he/she has said to me
- It makes me feel good to think about him/her
- Nothing else in the whole wide world matters compared to him/her
- I would do anything for him/her, even die
- I want to live as if this were my last day with him/her

Finally, consider this:

Would you do anything differently today if you knew this was your last day with God?

Let us never take His eternal love for granted! 

The Fifth Season

So bummed out today by the cold weather and dark days looming. Why can't God just let us have summer all the time? I could go for that (including year-round vacation)! 😆

We're told that God "changes the times and the seasons" (Daniel 2:21). And I'm sure there are plenty of scientific explanations for why this happens and perhaps even why it may be necessary.

In a similar way, life itself is a series of seasons. We each pass through four seasons of life, from birth (spring) to old age (winter). And as with the weather, each season of life has something difficult to help us grow, and something good to cherish. And if we stop long enough to notice, each season is a constant reminder of life and death.

If it all ended there, we would certainly have good reason to be depressed. But what if there was a *fifth season*?

A season only filled with life and goodness that never ended? Well, there is!

The same God who made the earth and keeps the seasons in motion has prepared a place for us that will only be filled with his life and goodness.

Just the way he intended us to live originally. But when we rebelliously turned our backs on him, we severed ourselves from our perfect relationship with him and his life, resulting in inevitable death.

Only by accepting the blood sacrifice of his Son Jesus in faith—a conscious choice—are we able to receive life and reconnect again to the loving Holy God who wanted us in the first place. ♥

I am not sure if there will be seasons, as we know them, in our heavenly home, but we can rest assured that this "fifth season" will be far beyond anything we can even imagine right now. Permanent and glorious! Summer vacation will pale in comparison! And back-to-school fall or winter storms will never haunt us again.

Now I can go for that! I hope you can too. 

"I go to prepare a place for you... that where I am, there you may be also." ~Jesus (John 14:2)

CHAPTER SIXTEEN

Timeless Promises

Prayer:

God of Hope, thank you for your precious promises! Please help us embrace your Word in our heart and soul, as you use it to strengthen our faith and hope in you.

Salvation

For God so loved the world that He gave His only begotten Son, that whoever believes in Him should not perish but have everlasting life. For God did not send His Son into the world to condemn the world, but that the world through Him might be saved. (John 3:16–17)

- ♥ But as many as received Him, to them He gave the right to become children of God, to those who believe in His name: who were born, not of blood, nor of the will of the flesh, nor of the will of man, but of God. (John 1:12–13)
- ♥ For the wages of sin *is* death, but the gift of God *is* eternal life in Christ Jesus our Lord. (Romans 6:23)
- ♥ . . . if you confess with your mouth the Lord Jesus and believe in your heart that God has raised Him from the dead, you will be saved. . . . For "whoever calls on the name of the Lord shall be saved." (Romans 10: 9,13)
- ♥ For by grace you have been saved through faith, and that not of yourselves; *it is* the gift of God, not of works, lest anyone should boast. (Ephesians 2:8–9)
- ♥ Jesus said to him, "I am the way, the truth, and the life. No one comes to the Father except through Me." (John 14:6)
- ♥ Jesus said to her, "I am the resurrection and the life. He who believes in Me, though he may die, he shall live. . . ." (John 11:25)
- ♥ . . . Believe on the Lord Jesus Christ, and you will be saved . . . (Acts 16:31)

Guidance

Trust in the LORD with all your heart,
    And lean not on your own understanding;
In all your ways acknowledge Him,

- And He shall direct your paths. (Proverbs 3:5–6)
- If any of you lacks wisdom, let him ask of God, who gives to all liberally and without reproach, and it will be given to him. (James 1:5)
- The fear of the LORD *is* the beginning of wisdom,
  And the knowledge of the Holy One *is* understanding.
  (Proverbs 9:10)
- For unto us a Child is born,
  Unto us a Son is given;
  And the government will be upon His shoulder.
  And His name will be called
  Wonderful, Counselor, Mighty God,
  Everlasting Father, Prince of Peace. (Isaiah 9:6)
- . . . when He, the Spirit of truth, has come, He will guide you into all truth; for He will not speak on His own *authority*, but whatever He hears He will speak; and He will tell you things to come. (John 16:13)
- Your word *is* a lamp to my feet
  And a light to my path. (Psalm 119:105)
- You will guide me with Your counsel,
  And afterward receive me to glory. (Psalm 73:24)
- You will show me the path of life;
  In Your presence *is* fullness of joy;
  At Your right hand *are* pleasures forevermore. (Psalm 16:11)

Peace

You will keep *him* in perfect peace,
Whose mind *is* stayed *on You*,
Because he trusts in You. (Isaiah 26:3)

- ♥ The eternal God *is your* refuge,
  And underneath *are* the everlasting arms . . .
  (Deuteronomy 33:27a)
- ♥ Therefore, having been justified by faith, we have peace with God through our Lord Jesus Christ ... (Romans 5:1)
- ♥ For you did not receive the spirit of bondage again to fear, but you received the Spirit of adoption by whom we cry out, "Abba, Father." (Romans 8:15)
- ♥ . . . the Spirit also helps in our weaknesses. For we do not know what we should pray for as we ought, but the Spirit Himself makes intercession for us with groanings which cannot be uttered. (Romans 8:26)
- ♥ Be anxious for nothing, but in everything by prayer and supplication, with thanksgiving, let your requests be made known to God; and the peace of God, which surpasses all understanding, will guard your hearts and minds through Christ Jesus. (Philippians 4: 6–7)
- ♥ I will both lie down in peace, and sleep;
  For You alone, O Lord, make me dwell in safety.
  (Psalm 4:8)
- ♥ Be content with such things as you have. For He Himself has said, "I will never leave you nor forsake you." (Hebrews 13:5)
- ♥ I can do all things through Christ who strengthens me. (Philippians 4:13)
- ♥ The Lord *is* my shepherd; I shall not want.
  He makes me to lie down in green pastures;

He leads me beside the still waters.
He restores my soul; He leads me in the paths of righteousness
For His name's sake.
Yea, though I walk through the valley of the shadow of death,
I will fear no evil; For You are with me;
Your rod and Your staff, they comfort me.
You prepare a table before me in the presence of my enemies;
You anoint my head with oil;
My cup runs over.
Surely goodness and mercy shall follow me
All the days of my life;
And I will dwell in the house of the LORD forever.
(Psalm 23)

♥ And He said to me, "My grace is sufficient for you, for My strength is made perfect in weakness." Therefore most gladly I will rather boast in my infirmities, that the power of Christ may rest upon me. (2 Corinthians 12:9)

♥ Peace I leave with you, My peace I give to you; not as the world gives do I give to you. Let not your heart be troubled, neither let it be afraid. ~Jesus (John 14:27)

♥ My people shall dwell in a peaceable habitation,
In secure dwellings, and in quiet resting places.
(Isaiah 32:18)

Hope

Blessed *is* the man who trusts in the LORD,
And whose hope is the LORD.
For he shall be like a tree planted by the waters,
Which spreads out its roots by the river,
And will not fear when heat comes;
But its leaf will be green,
And will not be anxious in the year of drought,
Nor will cease from yielding fruit. (Jeremiah 17:7–8)

♥ For since the beginning of the world
Men have not heard nor perceived by the ear,
Nor has the eye seen any God besides You,
Who acts for the one who waits for Him. (Isaiah 64:4)

♥ Oh, how great *is* Your goodness,
Which You have laid up for those who fear You,
Which You have prepared for those who trust in You
In the presence of the sons of men! (Psalm 31:19)

♥ For I consider that the sufferings of this present time are not worthy *to be compared* with the glory which shall be revealed in us. (Romans 8:18)

♥ He who did not spare His own Son, but delivered Him up for us all, how shall He not with Him also freely give us all things? . . . Who *is* he who condemns? *It is* Christ who died, and furthermore is also risen, who is even at the right hand of God, who also makes intercession for us. (Romans 8:32,34)

♥ For I am persuaded that neither death nor life, nor angels nor principalities nor powers, nor things present nor things to come, nor height nor depth, nor any other created thing, shall be able to separate us from the love of

God which is in Christ Jesus our Lord. (Romans 8:38–39)

- ♥ And the ransomed of the Lord shall return,
  And come to Zion with singing,
  With everlasting joy on their heads.
  They shall obtain joy and gladness,
  And sorrow and sighing shall flee away. (Isaiah 35:10)
- ♥ Our citizenship is in heaven, from which we also eagerly wait for the Savior, the Lord Jesus Christ, who will transform our lowly body that it may be conformed to His glorious body, according to the working by which He is able even to subdue all things to Himself. (Philippians 3:20–21)
- ♥ Blessed be the God and Father of our Lord Jesus Christ, who according to His abundant mercy has begotten us again to a living hope through the resurrection of Jesus Christ from the dead, to an inheritance incorruptible and undefiled and that does not fade away, reserved in heaven for you, who are kept by the power of God through faith for salvation ready to be revealed in the last time. (1 Peter 1:3–5)
- ♥ Beloved, now we are children of God; and it has not yet been revealed what we shall be, but we know that when He is revealed, we shall be like Him, for we shall see Him as He is. And everyone who has this hope in Him purifies himself, just as He is pure. (1 John 3:2–3)
- ♥ Let us hold fast the confession of our hope without wavering, for He who promised is faithful. (Hebrews 10:23)
- ♥ . . . looking for the blessed hope and glorious appearing of our great God and Savior Jesus Christ . . . (Titus 2:13)
- ♥ May the God of hope fill you with all joy and peace in believing, so that you may abound in hope by the power of the Holy Spirit. (Romans 15:13)

♥ Let not your heart be troubled; you believe in God, believe also in Me. In My Father's house are many mansions; if it were not so, I would have told you. I go to prepare a place for you. And if I go and prepare a place for you, I will come again and receive you to Myself; that where I am, there you may be also. ~Jesus (John 14:1–3) ♥

Epilogue of Hope

The Most Important Thing

If I could only share one message with you, this would be it.

The most important thing is to receive God's gift of salvation through Jesus, to know Him as our personal Savior and Lord forever.

How do we do this?

1. Acknowledge that sin tragically separates us from God, and we are powerless to heal that separation in our own strength.

2. Realize that the only one who can heal our broken relationship with God is the perfect Son of God, Jesus Christ, who paid our debt by his death and blood sacrifice on the cross. It is God's grace alone that saves us, as we choose to trust him and receive his gift.

3. Believe and receive by faith what God has said and done.

"For God so loved the world that He gave His only begotten Son, that whoever believes in Him should not perish but have everlasting life." (John 3:16)

Suggested Prayer:

Dear God, I know I have failed you in many ways, and I am truly sorry. I'm becoming more keenly aware of my desperate need for a Savior. And I'm realizing that Jesus is the only one who can save me! As the perfect Son of God, he has already paid for my sin when he died on the cross.

So today, right now, I'm trusting in your free gift of grace and loving forgiveness through the death of Jesus on the cross. I reach out in faith and call on your name for forgiveness and eternal salvation. Help me live close to you as I learn and grow in faith.

Amen. ♥

What Now?

You may ask, "Now that I am born again as God's child, how do I grow in my new faith?" Here's what helps me:

1. Feed your faith

Faith comes by hearing the Word of God. Get into the habit of reading your Bible every day, even if it's just a verse or two. And commit to memory those verses that are most meaningful. Pause often and thank him for saving you and making you a citizen of Heaven—and his very precious child.

2. Nurture your relationship with the Lord

Prayer is communicating with him, anytime and anywhere. Seek to know him, and open your heart fully to him. Humbly talk to him. Ask for what you need. Ask for forgiveness when you're aware of any sin. Thank him for all his blessings. Listen to his Holy Spirit inside you—messages of love, guidance, wisdom, and peace. Treasure the privilege of being his dearly loved child forever!

3. Live out your faith

As you discover in his Word more of who God is and the way he wants us to live, you'll begin to bear fruit: love, joy, peace, goodness, giving, compassion, patience, helping others, etc. Gathering together with other believers can be a much-needed lifeline. Remember that faith is not necessarily a feeling but a choice—a choice we make continually. Ask him to guide you and give you the faith and strength to walk the path he has for you, his very best just for you! And you'll soon find the joy of doing it all with him, and for him.

There is no greater hope!

About the Author

Welby O'Brien

Welby O'Brien holds a master's degree in counseling from Portland State University and a teaching degree from Biola University. She has published articles on CBN.com, *50Plus Magazine*, and *Charisma Magazine* and been a featured guest on TV, radio, and podcasts. Welby is a contributing author to *Chicken Soup for the Soul* and has also authored *Love Our Vets: Restoring Hope for Families of Veterans with PTSD*, *Goodbye for Now: Practical Help and Personal Hope for Those Who Grieve*, and *Formerly a Wife*.

Learn more at **WelbyO.com**

Welby O'Brien
GOODBYE
FOR NOW
Practical Help and
Personal Hope
for Those Who Grieve
"I know Goodbye for Now
will be a blessing and a help
to many, many people."
PAT ROBERTSON

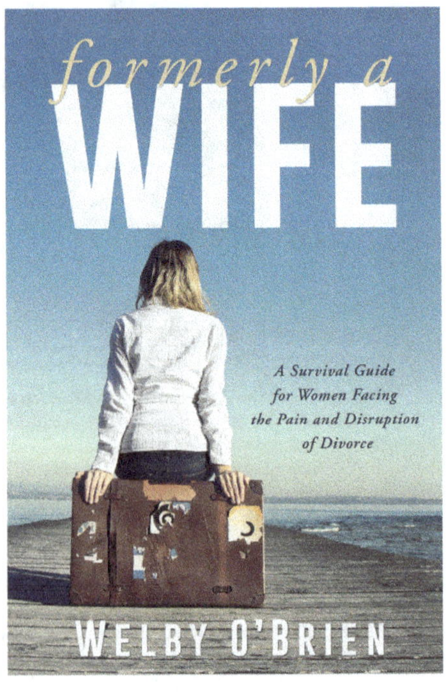
formerly a
WIFE
A Survival Guide
for Women Facing
the Pain and Disruption
of Divorce
WELBY O'BRIEN

WELBY O'BRIEN
REVISED EDITION
LOVE OUR VETS
Restoring Hope for Families of Veterans
with PTSD
"...a unique and valuable resource...
practical and emotional support to countless loved ones of veterans."
Suzanne Best, Ph.D. Co-author of Courage After Fire

Other Books by Welby O'Brien

Goodbye for Now:
Practical Help and Personal Hope for Those Who Grieve
This vital guide is an ideal combination of sensible advice and solid spiritual hope. This comprehensive faith-based resource not only tackles urgent, immediate tasks such as planning the service and handling financial matters but also offers help and hope for the long journey of healing ahead. *Goodbye for Now* will assist, comfort, and encourage those who are losing or have lost a loved one.

Formerly a Wife: A Survival Guide for Women Facing the Pain and Disruption of Divorce
Divorce is hard, and divorce can be especially challenging for women of faith. Written from both firsthand experience and a counselor's perspective, *Formerly a Wife* is a resource for women who are reeling from the devastation of divorce. It reveals practical steps toward survival, healing, and moving on. *Formerly a Wife* provides reassurance, comfort, appropriate humor, encouragement, and hope for newly divorced women.

Love Our Vets: Restoring Hope for Families of Veterans with PTSD: 2nd Edition
Answering more than 60 heartfelt questions, providing down-to-earth wisdom and much-needed tips for taking care of yourself, and sharing as a counselor and from her personal experience of living with a veteran battling PTSD, Welby O'Brien gives hope, encouragement, and practical help for families and loved ones who are caught in the wake of the trauma. *Love Our Vets* addresses a broad spectrum of issues and concerns and offers realistic wisdom from a wide variety of individuals who share from real hearts and lives.

Visit **WelbyO.com** to find all
these books and other helpful resources.

www.ingramcontent.com/pod-product-compliance
Lightning Source LLC
LaVergne TN
LVHW010858110826
845149LV00005B/1422
9781970897005